BACK TALK!

WOMEN LEADERS CHANGING THE CHURCH

Susan Willhauck

The Pilgrim Press
Cleveland

The Pilgrim Press
700 Prospect Avenue
Cleveland, Ohio 44115-1100
thepilgrimpress.com

10 09 08 07 06 05   5 4 3 2 1

Library of Congress Cataloging-in-Publication Data

Willhauck, Susan, 1955–
    Back talk! : women leaders changing the church / Susan Willhauck.
      p. cm.
    Includes bibliographical references and index.
    ISBN 0-8298-1653-4 (alk. paper)
    1. Christian leadership.   2. Women clergy.   3. Women church officers.
    4. Feminism—Religious aspects—Christianity. I. Title.
BV652.1.W489 2005
262'.1'082—dc22   2005022478

CONTENTS

PREFACE

THIS IS A BOOK THAT CELEBRATES the church and scans horizons poised for change. It applauds women's leadership in the church and suggests that women and men can and should speak out and act for change in the church. This book tells some stories of change that provide clues for effective leadership. It is a book that talks back to the church and advocates "back talk" as a viable and important methodology for doing theology and ministry. Women have a lot to say to the church, and their voices need to be heard. You may not agree with everything they say, but you will, I believe, be inspired and lured into dialogue with them. I have spent some time asking women leaders across the country and abroad what they celebrate about the church and what they would like to see changed. I talked with Baptists, Methodists, Lutherans, Quakers, Episcopalians, Anglicans, Presbyterians, and Roman Catholics in several countries. It was a great privilege to stand in the presence of women leaders in today's church. Their stories beg to be told and shared, attempting to overcome some of the denominational isolationism that is so pervasive. Those I interviewed responded to my questions with enthusiasm, wisdom, and passion. What they say is truly profound.

I have also talked with many men in the church, lay and ordained, leaders and "bystanders," as they sometimes called themselves. Mostly they appreciate and admire the leadership of women in the church and the changes that have come as a result of their leadership. They acknowledge, however, that the church has not always in all places affirmed women's leadership.

I believe that this is a *kairos* time in the church, when new, exciting things are happening. Some old ways are being replaced for the better. This book uses discourse, or ways of talking today to focus on the areas of change that are coming about in the church and that women are calling for with strong, clear voices. What they are asking for is not just about women or "women's issues" or justice for women. They are asking for change that will steer the church back on a truer course.

I once heard the saying, "There is the church, but then there is *the* church." This means that the most truthful manifestation of the church will always survive, will always be there, despite false and flawed or superficial versions. We have a responsibility, a duty, and a privilege to *lead* the church toward truly being the church God intended. That is what leadership is all about. It is not about being popular or charismatic or entertaining or successful. Leadership, particularly for women in these days, is about taking the wheel and navigating rough and rugged terrain, dodging some bullets, but always moving forward. It is not about running over people on the way, but more about picking up hitchhikers, welcoming the stranger, offering hospitality to the alien, befriending the have-nots. It is taking a dangerous risk to open the door to anyone who knocks.

The following pages contain the thoughts, prayers, dreams, and visions of some women and men leaders in ministry today. Some of these men and women are clergy, some lay. Some are students, some are young, some are old. Some have years of experience in the church. Some have very little. What they have in common is a call from God, a vocation, and a sense of purpose that makes them step forth in leadership.

I begin by explaining what back talk is and is not, and how it has and still does create change in the church. Chapter two examines areas for growth and change that are being called for in the church, what needs changing, and why. In chapter three I look at the biblical and historical sources (many of them feminist) for understanding back talk and its role in leadership. Chapter four contains narratives of how some women leaders have created change and introduces strategies for effective change. Chapter five addresses the limits of talk in bringing about change and the importance of "walking the walk" and putting the money where the mouth is. The final chapter reviews the strategies for how we work together on the "frontlines" to create change but still remain accountable to the church as the bearer of God's message of Good News to the world.

Although I have referred to myself as "tragically white," I have been greatly impacted by African American theologians and womanist scholars. I have been challenged and significantly awed and humbled by their courage in the struggle. Much of what is exciting in theory and studies on women's leadership in ministry, it seems, comes out of their ideas and work.

In this book I attempt to clearly identify the conceptual framework I am working in so that readers may argue with it. One of my pet peeves about academic writing is that scholars put their theories "out there" and are expected to defend them to the grave. If they are solid arguments, they'll hold up, the assumption goes. While scholars should put forth salient thoughts, such a static notion of the purpose of scholarship frustrates me. I have come to believe that the goal is more to frame the discussion, to raise the questions, provide some clues, and hopefully stimulate dialogue. In this vein, I hope readers will talk back to this book in order to further our understanding of leadership in the church.

ACKNOWLEDGMENTS

THERE ARE MANY PEOPLE I should acknowledge and thank. I want to thank students in the Women's Leadership in Ministry courses I have taught at Wesley Theological Seminary in Washington, D.C. The network of women and men to whom I spoke and asked for insight is vast. I thank all those who shared their stories, invited me into their homes, churches, and offices and allowed me to share them with my readers. These are all "real people," though I changed the names of some at their request. The participants in the study openly disclosed their joys and pain. I am grateful to the Association of Theological Schools and the Lilly Foundation for providing a research grant for this project. Several people were instrumental in lining up contacts for me: Jan Naylor Cope, Rev. Linda Rettenmeyer and Rev. Steve Rettenmeyer, and Rev. Kyunglim Shin Lee. I thank Rev. Margaret Jones and Rev. Chris Jones for their hospitality in England. I want to thank Dr. Denise Dombkowski Hopkins, Rev. Walt Westbrook, Rev. Dr. Debra J. Hanson, and Rev. Dr. Janice Jenkins for their help with several parts of the manuscript. I am also grateful to Howrtine Farrell Duncan, reference librarian at Wesley Theological Seminary, for her abounding resourcefulness. I hope to honor the memory of Dr. Sue Zabel, who lived and died with extraordinary chutzpa. Thanks also to the "other two wise women" for their friendship, and to Steve, Hannah, Bud, and Georgia (some All-Pro back talkers) for their patience.

As always I appreciate the support of my extended family. I dedicate this book to my mother, Betty Jean Yates Etheridge.

▪ 1 ▪

BACK TALK!

IN MANY WAYS, change is a constant and occurs without our asking for it. The world changes. People change. In the church, people come and go. Some mature in their faith, some drop out. As we learn new things about ourselves and our world, we change and the church changes with us. Good change that revitalizes the church does not solely come from our own efforts. Often, it comes despite our efforts! Indeed, Anthony de Mello once said, "Change that is real is change that is not willed." It comes from the work of the Holy Spirit. The Holy Spirit can transform even the most stagnant, the most hopelessly mired, conflicted, and unjust church! Yet good change can also come about from healthy and productive relationships among women and men who are identifying needed change and seeking it.[1]

Now, sometimes people do not like change. Even the most insignificant change in the church is like moving the furniture around in heaven. You are just not supposed to do that. People squirm and resist and talk about how much better the old way was. Change is painful, but it is also an opportunity for exquisite joy. There are many ways to ask for and create change. Linguistic studies have shown us how important language is. It may be the most distinctive human quality we possess, the ability to communicate that is essential to human societies. Language reflects our history and culture. It shapes us, and we are shaped by it. Language can hurt or it can heal. Linguists also acknowledge the limits of language, which I explore in chapter five. Communication is an enterprise broader than language, but language explains a lot about who we are, how we get things done, and where we are headed. I believe that one productive way of bringing renewal to the church is through a certain kind of talk.

What is Back Talk?

During my southern upbringing, my mother frequently said to me, "Don't you talk back to me!" Or, she would say, "Don't you sass me, 'chile'," meaning, "don't give me any lip," meaning, "do as you're told with no questions asked!" Back talk is traditionally thought of as rude and impertinent behavior. My mother was one of twelve children, and I was one of twenty-seven grandchildren. So back talk, regardless of the admonitions against it, was prevalent in my family. Admittedly, I was somewhat of an insolent child (and I haven't changed much!), but the message was clear. You are a child, so you are not supposed to question my authority. Now I should say that my mother is a dear soul, and although steeped in the "old school" of child rearing, she was always a loving and devoted parent. She taught me to respect authority, if not always to acquiesce to it. She came to know, however, that God had put an unquenchable curiosity and utterly relentless spirit in her only daughter. She found out that talking back was my specialty (everyone has a gift!). She learned that it did no good to tell me to stop talking back, so she taught me how to talk back with respect and love. So I talked back, and she listened patiently, with gentle firmness, good humor, and grace.

Even as I heard my parents say, "Don't give me any back talk!" I have also heard the church say it. Too many times women in ministry are told that in order to get ahead, in order to succeed in ministry, you have to play by the rules, just do as you are told and do not question. Do not be a troublemaker if you want to get anywhere. I propose in this book that back talk, which people usually consider to be a negative, rude, and disrespectful thing, has its place and may actually be a positive dynamic for change. I have observed and learned that talking back can be done in such a way that the church will listen. I advocate a kind of feminist linguistic model and methodology for leadership that creates positive change. Linguists talk about words that are *polysemitic*—meaning one thing *and* another, or having multiple meanings simultaneously. So back talk has at least two meanings, one as insolent, impertinent questioning, and the other as language that creates change. Or, maybe this is really the same meaning! The church, if it is truly the church, is a kind and instructive parent that allows and listens to honorable back talk. Back talk can be virtuous and respectful because it demonstrates that someone cares. If a person does not care or love something, then there is no need to talk back to it. If we did not care, we would not be wasting our breath! Instead of walking away, we are talking back.

Feminist writer bell hooks deserves the credit for first identifying "talking back" as a response to oppression and as a method to empower change. Mostly, language has been a weapon of the powerful, but it can be a political, iconoclastic activity. She gave birth to an idea that now has a life of its own. She wrote:

> In the world of the southern black community I grew up in, "back talk" and "talking back" meant speaking as an equal to an authority figure. It meant daring to disagree and sometimes it just meant having an opinion. In the old school, children were meant to be seen and not heard....To speak then when one was not spoken to was a courageous act—an act of risk and daring.[2]

I want to demonstrate how back talk is a courageous and daring act that yields results and is vital for the Christian community. Back talk is certainly not the only way to create change, but I believe it is one way, a good way that change has and will come to pass.

The Post-feminist Predicament

There is a rather alarming view that the women's movement is over and done with, that it is "old news," and since women have broken into most of the male-dominated professions, including the ministry, there is no need for "radical feminist" ideas and challenges. In 1989 Danielle Crittenden interviewed young female college students and asked them if they were feminists. She reported that most of the young women seemed "rather ungratefully bored by the whole thing." Many reacted quite negatively to the term feminist "as if it were an orange, bell-bottomed pantsuit found at the back of their mother's closet." Even so, according to Crittenden, these young women were still feminists in the sense that they thought women should be able to do anything they want to do and should not be held back or denied anything because of their gender.[3] It seems they took for granted the victories without experiencing or appreciating the struggle, and the term "feminist" is pejorative. Even in 2002, a young woman about to graduate from college was interviewed for a local newspaper. Asked if she was a feminist, she responded, "I don't need that. I feel like can do anything I set my mind to. That was my mother's issue." The positive aspect of what she says is that women *have* made gains in society that have made it possible for younger women not to have to fight the same old battles. Yet, her remarks reveal a lack of a sense of history and little understanding of the struggle of those who came before her. I wonder if she will feel the same way when she experiences discrimination or harassment in the workplace.

The young women today grew up with Title 9 and feminism "like fluoride in the water," according to Joanna Starek, who teaches women's studies at the University of Colorado. But our institutions have not necessarily changed. It may be difficult for them to believe sexism and harassment and sexual assault still exists, but it does.[4] When women want to do things they are "not supposed to do," such as go to The Citadel, become a sportscaster, or play football, they become acutely aware of the strength of the resistance.

The strides made by women in leadership in the church are impressive, but the need for change is far from over. We live in what Frances Mascia-Lees and Patricia Sharpe call the predicament of post-feminism, referring to a context in which the feminism of the 1970s is suspect and balkanized.[5] It is a context of "backlash," to use the term coined by Susan Faludi to express negative reactions to gains made by women where women have found an ear in the press for attacking other feminists.[6] Some felt the feminist agenda was fulfilled. Critics cried, "Get over it." Feminism was watered down to self-help and self-esteem, i.e., "all women really need is confidence and to feel good about themselves." Even women who still acknowledge a commitment to feminism may admit that while helping to positively develop women's critical consciousness, it ironically led women of various cultural backgrounds to question feminist theory. Their newfound consciousness may have allowed them to name and define their own oppression and respond against white feminism. The debates became internal, fragmented, and predictable, diminishing feminists' ability to offer real criticism and insight.

Carter Heyward describes the situation well in *Staying Power: Reflections on Gender, Justice, and Compassion*:

> I am especially concerned today that many white feminist women, like our white male allies, have become so attached to the liberal notion of the individual "self"—self growth, personal recovery, and the psychologizing of all our pain and troubles, that we are giving up our sacred power to participate

in changing the world: not just our own personal world or the social world in which we're most comfortable with, those who think like us and act like us and understand us, but the whole world of many cultures, colors, beliefs, complexities and contradictions.[7]

It seems that we live in an age of "posts," post-this, post-that, post-modern, post-toasties. We are living beyond everything we have ever known. It is not possible to turn back the clock, but it is important to remember where we came from and where we have been as we navigate a so-called post-feminist world. Women should not shrink from our commitment and struggle, even as we come to define it in new ways. As Rebecca Chopp has claimed, the basic tenets of feminist theology are no longer for women only (and a few sympathetic men), but intrinsic to Christianity.[8] In a multicultural world, varied theologies, including black theology, feminist, womanist, *mujerista, minjung,* Native American, African, and Asian theologies, are resources for leadership in the church.

Need for New Kinds of Leadership

The study of leadership is emerging as a vast, multidisciplinary enterprise. Contextual leadership in business, politics, science, education, the arts, religion, and many other spheres is fertile ground for intellectual debate about shaping culture. It seems that almost everyone is weighing in on what is effective, where we ought to be going, and the wave of the future. Barbara Kellerman, executive director of the Center for Public Leadership at Harvard's John F. Kennedy School of Government, comments that scholars in traditional academic disciplines are often suspicious of work that is multidisciplinary, such as leadership studies, because they are more used to "digging deep" than "scanning wide."[9] However, in many disciplines there is a growing awareness of the need to connect theory with practice, to link the principles of the discipline with what it means to live in today's society. This is especially true in theological education. It is less helpful to convey abstract concepts divorced from the day-to-day questions we face. In all fields of theological education, we have to ask what kind of leadership is needed for our religious institutions of today and tomorrow.

From observation and experience, and from talking with people in the church, I can say with confidence that much of the current leadership in the church takes its cue from the American political ethos of our country's prosperous decades. A good leader has been seen as a party-liner, someone who can rally people around the "party." A good leader is supposed to have a vision, but that vision needs to be in line with the success of the church as the "party" defines it. One traditionally successful leader is the "benevolent dictator" who, through the strength of his or her character and charisma, can get people to do just about anything he or she needs or wants. This leader is well loved (even idolized in some cases) and followed without question. If the country (church) is prosperous (growing, successful), this leader can get away with just about anything, including immoral behavior by just about any standards. Now it is good to be loved. Some people go into the ministry because they want to be loved. Though that kind of leader may succeed on the surface, usually he or she has a stake in the status quo, and one could sincerely ask how that leader has made a mark in the world for God. We also are familiar with the "top-down," command and control leadership of positional power. Everyone else in the organization tends to be either a "bottom feeder," gulping everyone who gets in the way of upward mobility, or a "bottom-dweller," those conditioned or forced to stay on the bottom.

I have known my share of such leaders, and these types of leadership have run their course for at least two reasons: (1) Society is more diverse, and some cultures and peoples do not relate to that kind of leadership; and (2) The continuance of the church depends upon a leadership that is not about governing a "fiefdom" but about extending beyond the doors of the church.

Even though, from the standpoint of the status quo, the needs of the church have changed, leaders who do not "work the crowd," who do not strive to please but rock the boat, are often punished (even martyred). Leaders who think outside the box, who do things differently, are not seen as team players. This is especially evident in language. It is difficult in a hierarchical system to speak as an equal to authority figures as bell hooks suggested. Carter Heyward offers this reproach:

A common distortion of God's voices as historically they have been transmitted in the church is that it is one voice spoken "from above." It is spoken "down" to us; the voice of the Pope, the Bishop, the priest, the preacher, the

President, the one in charge. Even when spoken as a benevolent voice, this hierarchical power, insofar as it represents an unchanging, static relationship between God and his/her people or between the priest and his/her people is not a sacred voice at all but rather that of an idol created to hold patriarchal power in place.[10]

The church has sometimes seemed to be like a ventriloquist, throwing its voice onto puppets, pretending to speak for the voiceless and powerless. We've got to get a new act. Rebecca Chopp agrees: "Women will be forever strangers unless their words and their voices revise the social and symbolic rules of language, transforming the law of ordered hierarchy in language, in subjectivity, and in politics into a grace of rich plentitude for human flourishing."[11]

Women are speaking, and not with rented words. They are not speaking in the voice of someone else in order to fit in, but in their own way. Marjorie Procter-Smith has affirmed the use of *heteroglossia,* two or more voices other than those of the dominant language. These other languages are coming into legitimacy as an alternative to univocal speech.[12]

Excitingly, there is a growing movement or breed of church leaders who are speaking up and creating change. While I have found no way to actually scientifically document the existence of any kind of organized cadre of avant-garde new leaders, their presence is being made known in many ways—through the work they do, their spirituality, and their influence on the church and community. These leaders are not just following the latest fads in ministry and church growth doctrine. While there is little empirical evidence that gender differences in attitudes and behaviors can account for success or effectiveness in leadership, I did find people suggesting that women's leadership is making a difference, particularly in the church. Some studies such as one conducted by the Foundation for Future Leadership have found superior performance by women leaders in many professional spheres. Deborah L. Rhode, professor of law at Stanford, attributes women's superiority over their male counterparts to having to overcome extreme obstacles and being held to higher standards than men.[13]

This reality is in direct contradiction to the view that if a woman "makes it," the standards must be lower. John R. Matthews of The Midwest Ministry Development Service, a career center associated with the

Lutheran Church, found in a study of women ministerial candidates that significant and positive changes taking place in the ministry are most likely caused by the way women perceive and carry out their ministries:

> From our vantage point at the Career Center, significant changes in the nature of ministry *are* taking place. There is also a logical connection between those changes and ways women candidates perceive their ministries that are different from how men in ministry view what they are doing. Professions and the nature of professionals that populate them change slowly. It takes momentous upheaval to change either the image or the heart of a profession. Nevertheless, our data and clinical impressions tell us that the heart, and possibly the image, of ministry is changing. Also, there are many strikingly positive benefits both for the church and for the life of clergy that accompany those changes.[14]

In *Beyond the Dark Night: A Way Forward for the Church?* Mary C. Grey describes new models of authority and leadership, brought by women to the playing field, that are serving to break the deadlock in the church.[15] I would add a caution against assuming one distinctive female style, yet talking with people has convinced me she is right. Barbara Troxell and Patricia Farris document their claim that women contribute to the renewal of the United Methodist Church, but their contributions are either overlooked or perceived as threatening.[16] These catalysts for change can teach us something about leadership, about ecclesiology, about spirituality, and about direction for the mission of the church.

This book is about women creating change and talking back, but I found that in good conscience, I really could not leave out the voices of the men "back talkers." They too are a crucial part of this new breed of leaders. I found huge reservoirs of support for women in ministry from men. I include some of their contributions to change in the church. When I began this research, however, I focused on how women were talking back and collectively speaking out for justice in the church. I knew, of course, that women have been talking back to the church for a long time, but I am suggesting that now is the time for women to really engage wholeheartedly in back talk, to "hunker down" and speak out and act collectively for change. And the church needs to listen to us with an ear inclined to hear.

Women in the Church

Women make up the vast majority of church members and churchgoers in America. According to a 1999–2000 poll from the George Barna Research Group, 10 percent more women than men attend church (45 percent of women and 35 percent of men).[17] More women than men are actively involved in a Bible study class or engage in devotional practices. According to Princeton Religious Research Center's *Religion in America,* more church members are women.[18] Yet the leadership is overwhelmingly still male. According to *Emerging Trends,* "Women have consistently been more likely than men to belong to churches. This has been true for every measurement taken over the last six decades."[19]

"Women have always been church" and represent the majority of active Christians today, yet the church is "publicly visible as a male institution," according to James F. Kay.[20] Mark Chaves has noted the irony in the fact that women have occupied and continue to occupy significant leadership roles within denominations that officially prohibit them from occupying such roles.[21] Diana L. Hayes expresses this problem as it appears in the black church. Historically, women have been the backbone of the black church. Ironically, black women have had little formal leadership or office, though "not for lack of trying."[22] Delores C. Carpenter found that there are 2.5 to 3 females for every male in the black church, yet fewer than 5 percent of clergy in the historically black denominations are female.[23] Theologian Kwok Pui-lan asserts that in Asian churches, women are usually the majority, but they are marginalized in the power structure and in the congregation.[24] What's wrong with this picture? The church today is an organization controlled by men. Most of the senior pastors in Protestant churches are male (90 percent). Obviously, only 10 percent are female.[25] The majority of denominational leadership is also male. Even though most clergy are male, women in ministry do not have a proportionate stake in the leadership. This is the glass ceiling. The last twenty-five years have brought many changes in terms of the number of women accepted into the ordained ministry in Protestant denominations, according to John R. Matthews. He quotes Susan E. Nagle: "It took us more than 19 centuries to take the step that included me. We might say that in the whole history of the church and of the ordained ministry from Pentecost to the present, only slightly over 1% of that time has known the sustenance and encouragement of the ordination of women."[26]

Matthews's impression is that the experience of women in ministry has been different from that of men in at least one significant regard: "There has been continuous resistance to their being there." Sometimes the resistance is subtle, sometimes it is blatant, but that resistance is a constant.[27] There is a temptation (though it may be unspoken in some cases) to associate a perceived decline in mainline Protestantism with the increase of women's leadership, effectively blaming women for a loss of members. Actually, many sociologists of religion are noting a promising upturn in the importance of religion in the lives of Americans, and some believe that women's leadership may be a factor in that spiritual renewal.

In mainline Protestant traditions we sometimes take the ordination of women for granted. It seems hard to believe that for centuries women were denied and rejected by the church and that, in most cases, were granted ordination only a relatively few years ago. Though women still exercised leadership in the church, they were and still are held back. A parody by Gracia Fay Ellwood entitled "Should Men Be Ordained," first published in the magazine *Daughters of Sarah,* reverses arguments used against women's ordination and calls into question denying leadership based on gender:

> Spurred by the sight of various oppressed groups calling for liberation and equality, men are now demanding admission to the ordained ministries on an equal footing with women. While their claims are not totally without merit, I hope to show on the basis of Scripture and traditional Christian practice why their admission would not be appropriate at present. Any Christian knows why men have not been ordained to the ministry. They belong to the Ruling Club. Men represent secular power; nearly all societies and governments have been and are presently patriarchal. Any Christian can observe that men run things—or if they don't, they get credit for it. Which is exactly why a man makes a poor representative to a Christian sacramental or preaching ministry. . . . [Jesus] commissioned women to be the first apostles—that is, witnesses of his resurrection. When a woman preaches, she is herself a living testimony to a God who turns Nobody into Somebody.[28]

Even though it is exaggerated, as parodies often are, this piece points to the injustice of exclusion that women have felt from the church. Some have experienced this pain so intensely that they have left, seeking alternative

communities of faith. Others stay in the church and try to reform or transform it. One woman expressed her own mandate for leadership thusly:

> I think that women should not ask for permission, but simply do. Whatever
> it is the Holy Spirit calls you to do, do it! I am a priest by my baptism into
> Jesus and grace of the Holy Spirit. We don't need women in Roman collars
> and robes, titled, working to be bishop, cardinal, and politicizing to be pope.
> We need women filled with the Holy Spirit to *be* Jesus where they *are*.[29]

Yet other women do want the church to recognize their leadership, and
they seek out that recognition and the sanctity that the church confers on
its leaders, according to some theologies. While there has been an increase
of women in leadership positions in the church, that increase has not been
proportionate to the numbers of women involved in the church. According
to the Barna Research Group, the Christian spirituality of America depends
on women. Webminister.com reports: "Men are the senior pastors of more
than nine out of ten Protestant churches (and, of course, 100% of Catholic
Churches). However, a new nationwide survey from the Barna Research
Group suggests that women shoulder most of the responsibility for the
health and vitality of the Christian faith in the country."[30]

This study shows the importance of women to the spiritual climate of
the United States. Women are also at the heart of the church in Africa, in
Latin America, and in Russia, according to many news reports and stories
coming from these parts of the world.

Here is the problem. If women make up the majority of the church, why
aren't more women in positions of authority and decision making? Some
would still argue it is because women are not called to ministry and should
not be in leadership, but instead work behind the scenes. Others would say
that it is not that women are not called—indeed, history records a chorus
of voices celebrating women's call to ministry—but many may have stifled
that voice within because is was not culturally acceptable for them to be
ministers, or that they have somehow otherwise been prevented from fulfilling that call.

The second half of this problem is why aren't there more men in the
pews? Men have not left the church recently because of women's leadership, as some have suggested. No polls that I have seen support any recent
exodus on the part of men. On the contrary, many men highly respect

women pastors. Questioning the status quo is not to say that women want to take over the church. Women just want proportionate investment in the leadership structure. We want men in the church, and we want good male leadership. The goal is not to take something away from men. There is a concern about the historic lack of men in the church. Is religious faith perceived as being a women's thing? Why are more women than men involved in church activities, worship and devotional practices? I am aware of male leaders in the church who share openly about their spirituality and are splendid models. We need more of them. Still, the issue of women's leadership and women's role in the church is not resolved. It sounds obvious to say that we need good women and men leaders to create change that is needed. The church as depicted at Pentecost is inclusive. Yet how inclusive are we? Although women account for half of the U.S. adult population, they represent a majority of religiously active individuals in twelve out of thirteen religious activities examined.[31]

Women have not had an overwhelming number of role models in leadership positions to inspire their leadership. The lack of women in formal leadership positions in the church mirrors society. Deborah L. Rhode points out that it is no secret that for most of recorded history women were excluded from formal leadership positions. A comprehensive review of encyclopedia entries on women leaders identified only about 850 famous or infamous women of eminence throughout the entire preceding two thousand years. Few of these women came to leadership on their own but through their relationship with men. Rhode contends that women are still dramatically underrepresented in top positions of authority.[32]

Some believe the disparity is a result of cultural lag and that it is just a matter of time until women catch up. This theory assumes that when women have been in the pipeline long enough and have earned their stripes, they will naturally assume more leadership. Progress, however, is not inevitable. The pipeline theory cannot explain the under-representation of women leaders in fields where nearly half or more of new entries for the field have been women for three or four decades.[33] Former Harvard president Larry Summers told a group of academics that women are under-represented in math and science fields because their gender makes them less apt for such careers. His misguided opinion initiated a tidal wave of criticism and may have cost him his job. Insinuating that gender differences mean that women may be less intellectually capable is incongruous.

Gender differences do not mean that women have to settle for less.

According to Sheron Patterson, "if women do not see themselves in leadership positions, they subconsciously assume that they should not and cannot lead."[34] The lack of role models and lack of visibility of women is gradually changing, and the few are speaking out to create change and increase power for women. Now for some, power is an ugly word, synonymous with manipulation and greed. Yet power is energy and necessary to get things done. Carolyn Heilbrun connects speech and power. She writes: "Power is the ability to take one's place in whatever discourse is essential to action and the right to have one's point matter."[35] Women have earned that right and power to a certain degree, but they will not and cannot settle for less than their full say and participation in the leadership of the church.

Positions vs. Leadership

More women in the hierarchy is not the only answer. Barbara Kellerman cautions against the assumption that having more women in positions of authority would be, ipso facto, good. Too many women produces the pink-collar ghetto such as in nursing and teaching where, she claims, high numbers of women seem to diminish the importance of these professions.[36] Sometimes women in leadership roles like being "the only woman" or enjoy the attention of being one of a few models and don't want to share the limelight with more women in lofty positions. Many women perceive a fixed number of female slots. Only a few women can be allowed to succeed as if they were men. Women become exceptionally good at finding ways of holding other women at bay.[37] But why should the presence of women diminish a profession? Perhaps we will get to the point where we can see that women in positions of leadership enhance a profession and increase public opinion toward it.

Leadership is, of course, not just about holding formal positions. More women in what is known in hierarchical parlance as "high level" positions is not the only way (or even the best way) to bring about change. As one student put it, why buy in to a male-created structure for power? Rebecca Chopp observed that solving the theological problem of patriarchy is not simply a matter of politely letting others in. More fundamental changes are needed in structures that will allow for multiplicity of ideas and styles of leadership.[38]

Kellerman suggests that women who find or derive meaning in life in ways and in things different from the way men find meaning may not place a high value on climbing the "greasy pole" to the top. Moreover, flattened organizational hierarchies, shared leadership, and the decline of authority mean that formal leadership is less important than it once was.[39] Indeed, many women and men believe that the most effective way to bring about change in the church, to shape the future of the church, is at the grassroots level. I believe this is true. This does not preclude or eliminate better representation for women in the formal leadership of the church. In this study I found that women are making a difference in the church, and having more women with proven effectiveness in leadership in decision-making positions could help to further advance needed change in the church.

We should not forget that groups of laywomen have been exercising tremendous leadership for years. Women's leadership and ability to bring about change in the global church is not dependent solely upon ordination or even equal treatment and full acceptance. These things are, however, critically important, and to say they don't matter is to say that it is okay for women to be held back. Kwok Pui-lan writes:

> Asian feminist theologians who support women's ordination do not advocate a clerical-hierarchical model of the church. They do not advocate women's ordination so that women may have a fair share in the power of domination in the church hierarchy. They advocate women's ordination so that women who are called by God may have the freedom and opportunity to exercise power—with others to equip the whole congregation. For them the purpose of women's ordination is not to allow women admission into the "male club," and the opportunity to perform "men's roles." They believe that women should not be contented with admission to the lowest rungs of church hierarchy. . . . Instead they envisage women seeking ordination to enlarge the church's vision of ministry.[40]

Delores C. Carpenter defends the professional model of ministry as it becomes more readily available to black women and other marginalized groups because there is a need for full-time, well-educated clergy.[41] As we work to find alternatives to a hierarchical way of being the church, women and men can claim their voices and their power from the margins. There is a tremendous challenge in adapting to succeed within an institution without losing the capacity to change it.

Talking in Church

When I was a teenager, a group of us youth would always sit together in church on the back pew. We would regularly get in trouble for whispering and giggling during the service. Once my mother turned around, pointed her finger at us, and said, "Now I know you girls know that there is no talking in church!" I am reminded of the often misunderstood Pauline injunction against women talking in church. Women and men, of course, *do* talk in church, and that is one of the positive ways that we live faithfully in community. I admire the Baptist tradition of my grandmother, where people had no problem talking back to the preacher. In *Church in the Round: Feminist Interpretation of the Church,* Letty Russell describes "table talk" as action and reflection of the church. Table talk has always been a way that the church has been the church—a way of sharing when we are gathered as a community. Table fellowship, the sharing of the Lord's Supper, nourished us to go into the world and bring the gospel to a starving, hurting world.[42] She points to bell hooks, whom I cited earlier, as a feminist who calls our attention to claiming a voice in the public sphere to confidently engage in the dialogue to interpret what it means to be a Christian. For Russell, we need to talk back to the tradition and no longer accept a patriarchal paradigm that places everything in a "hierarchy of domination and subordination, accepting the marginalization of the powerless as a given." Although in this paradigm the names and faces may change, it still continues to define women as marginal to the male center, still defines the female leader by male standards.[43]

Letty Russell describes talking back as a constant movement, spiral-like, which connects scripture and tradition with our human contexts. It is a dialogue, not a shouting match. I want to make it clear here, as I do throughout this book, that back talk is a dangerous thing. It should not be undertaken lightly. As Rev. Peggy Johnson pointed out, if you sass, you are liable to "get beat up double." Sometimes an oppressed minority will take sides with the oppressor against the back talker. Yet defiant speech is often necessary for leadership and change. Marjorie Procter-Smith says we must transform the "language of the rulers to the language of the whole free people of God." She compares this kind of language to sourdough bread starter, in that it is a "starter of hope."[44] Talking back, according to bell hooks, is a "rite of initiation," testing our courage while at the same time strengthening our commitment, preparing us for the future.[45]

In *The Web of Women's Leadership,* Jacqulyn Thorpe and I offer a positive metaphor of the web as an alternative to command and control, hierarchical leadership. I am sure that there are other effective metaphors and styles of leadership. I have seen some of these among the people I have talked with for this book. Back talk is not just a reaction but a way of leading or a methodology and a way of being the church. It is not an aggressive, confrontative, conflict-ridden, "asking for trouble" way of being. It is not rehearsing old wounds and swapping horror stories. Back talk or talking back is questioning, challenging, problem solving, and a moving forward kind of leadership. It is the dialogue that has to take place, though sometimes difficult, for positive change. Who are the "back talkers" and what do they do?

- Back talkers speak out about injustice within and outside the church. They do not give up when told no or "that's just the way it is."

- Back talkers know that their energy, their motivation, their ability comes from God.

- Back talkers have a spirit of humility. They know they may not always be right. They prayerfully strive to discern the difference between their opinion and wishes and God's will.

- Back talkers do not use sass, wit, or sarcasm in a hurtful way to get the better of someone. Rather they lovingly cause us to look at something from a different perspective.

- Back talkers do not pontificate, get up on a soapbox, or spout off their views. They talk back in actions as well as words. In fact, they know that words may not even be used at all in back talking. Their protest is in the way they live their lives as much as in what they say.

- Back talkers are not just chatting, whining, or engaged in idle, fruitless, back-and-forth, getting-nowhere discussion. Their talk is purposeful, measured, and a learning experience.

- Back talkers do not engage in or listen to gossip. Back talk does not involve the practice of backstabbing. Back talk is above board, done face-to-face.

Dennis Jacobson writes about agitation, which he defines as an act of love. For movers and shakers, agitation is "a vehicle for summoning forth the best from their leaders." I think of the agitation cycle in my old washing machine, chugging away. It is a means of getting others to act out of their own power and out of their own sense of what is right. It is not a way of getting someone to do what I want him or her to do, but it helps people discern and act out of their own vision. Relationship, he says, is a prerequisite of agitation. The same is true of back talk. It is done in community; in fact, agitation and back talk create community and build organizations, raising up good leaders. Jacobson writes: "Most churches do not operate on the basis of healthy agitation that is rooted in relationship and that summons forth the best from the people. They operate instead on the basis of manipulation, authoritarianism or guilt-tripping."[46]

Jesus *was* a great agitator, and I look at examples of back talk from scripture and tradition in chapter three. Some institutional structures, which limit the church's ability to embody the Gospel and engage in incarnational ministry (what Darrell Guder refers to as "institutional captivities") are being challenged today by back talk.[47] To talk back may be to challenge the status quo or to point out an injustice. It may mean dissenting from the teachings of one's tradition. Most churches have an established, essential set of beliefs, doctrines, confessions, or articles. In addition, they may have principles and other positions on certain moral issues. The Roman Catholic Church professes a belief in the infallibility of the church and of the Pope as the church's representative. There is some debate about the conditions set forth by the Vatican Councils required for a teaching to be infallible. This does not mean that all church teachings are up for grabs. It is possible, however, if one's own conscience dictates, to disagree or dissent.

In the Roman Catholic Church, if people in public positions such as priests or teachers or theologians dissent, they are urged by the magisterium to exercise great caution and in most cases to keep their dissent private. In reformed denominations, dissent is more common and public. For example, there has been much press about groups who disagree with their denomination's stand on the ordination of homosexuals. Theological and political diversity is common in many mainline denominations. The question becomes *how* one dissents. Does one dissent with intolerance or even violence?

The Good News movement in The United Methodist Church dissents publicly (often through the vehicle of the *Good News Magazine*). I believe in their right to dissent and in the obligation of the organization to publicly speak out. On the occasions where I have read the *Good News Magazine,* however, I find many examples of mean-spirited tactics used that go beyond disagreeing or dissenting to personal vendettas and verbal violence. A Presbyterian Church USA staffer, noted similarly of conservative splinter groups in her denomination that sabotaged denominationally sanctioned women's groups because of their so-called "feminist" bent by introducing legislation to cut their funding.[48] Political manipulation to try to discredit another group because you disagree with them is not fair play and not good back talk. Rosemary Ruether and Eleanor McLaughlin say that women operating from a stance of "radical obedience" rather than from one of dissent are more likely to make headway in male dominated institutions. That has not always been true. They acknowledge that "loyal dissent" is necessary to loosen rigidity in structures of domination.[49] Many people who favor ordination for women in the Roman Catholic Church do not think of themselves as dissenters, but have coined the term "benevolent subversives" to describe their work toward building a community that will live up to Jesus' ideals.

According to Darrell Guder:

> The community which is continually being converted makes every effort to maintain the "unity of the Spirit in the bond of peace" (Ephesians 4:3). Precisely when there are disagreements within the community, it incarnates the gospel by grappling with these problems and remaining united in Christ. Disagreeing *Christianly* [italics mine] is one of the most powerful forms of incarnational witness the church can practice.[50]

If one dissents too much, goes over the edge, should one then leave the church? I argue that if a person in good faith disagrees with his or her church's stand on any issue or teaching, he or she should speak out and find a way to talk back without walking away. Yet, again, that dissent and back talk should be carefully and prayerfully executed.

I am not just talking about empty words. Sheron Patterson writes about "walking counter culture," which is an act of movement against the grain. Such walking is actually a strut. It involves doing what women, according to prevailing sentiment, are not supposed to do, such as go to seminary in some traditions. In order to speak and act on our own terms she coaches us:

> We must move counter-culture. Let's move. Let's strut. We must strut. We can't crawl—that's for babies. We can't walk—this is the twenty-first century. Walking is an ancient mode of operation. Therefore, we strut. We take our time but keep moving. We strut, placing one foot in front of the other, we keep moving. Swing those arms. Lean back. Tilt the head, cock the chin, sweep the butt. Strut to the rhythm of some finger-popping Christian tune. Focus on the music. Focus on your steps. Focus on your God and the power that God gives you. And let us strut toward what we can be in the name of Jesus Christ.[51]

I invite us to hone in on what we say and do in the church today to strut our way forward.

▪ 2 ▪

HOLY CONVERSATIONS, HOLY CHANGE

THERE IS INDEED A LOT OF RHETORIC about leadership in the church today and a plethora of opinions about what kind of leadership is needed. Recent book titles reveal the spectrum of views about the most effective leadership. They range from *The Leadership Secrets of Attila the Hun* (I'm not kidding, that is the real title of a book) to *The Tao of Leadership.*[1] Is leadership defiantly swimming upstream or swimming with the flow of the people? Is it both? What kind of leadership is most needed for today's church? Some leaders in the corporate world and others with expertise in leadership in various organizations agree that leadership and the demands for leaders have changed. According to Jay Congar, "We no longer live in a world where we have the right to expect authorities to know the answers."[2]

The challenges of living in today's world require not simply application of expertise but adapting minute by minute to varying needs, attitudes, and values. We may know this in our heads, but we continue to operate as if top-level managers and leaders will provide success.[3] We crave easy answers. Even in the church we look for deliverance from on high, and I don't mean God here. We expect a perfect, charismatic pastor to come to our churches and make them successful. Yet, as Congar says happens in the world of business management, "If their magic fails, we kill them off." Some blame the seminaries for not forming effective pastors and leaders. Others blame the denominations for ordaining the wrong people. Neither the seminaries nor judicatories are perfect, but the new literature on leadership suggests to us that blame is not the answer, but changing our expectations about leadership may be.

Despite the confusion about what constitutes good and inspiring leadership for the church today, I have looked around and see examples of it everywhere. Examples that I believe ought to be shared, reflected upon, and emulated. Leadership that works in thriving churches these days is leadership for change. A thriving church is not necessarily a successful church by common standards, but one that is excited about its ministry and about doing the work of the gospel in the world. It is one with meaningful worship that is joyful, but more than a "feel good" experience. It is one that finds ways to share the message of the Christian faith in a pluralistic world. It is one that offers community and challenge to the people of God. A thriving church does not operate from a professional (expertise) model of ministry but from a spirit-filled people and leadership for change. It is not a maintenance-mode style of leadership, moving steadily along the same path, but a leadership that talks back, that engages in holy conversations with itself and with the world, dialogue that engenders true reflection and action.

Most of these examples of leadership for change in thriving churches and ministry settings come from women leaders, and these are the ones I focus on, not because men are not leading effectively, but because few people have really scrutinized the uniqueness of women's leadership and the gender factors in the changes that women have brought.

Talking about Change

Do I dare claim that back talk is holy talk? Theological foray into back talk may shed some light. Creation itself came from God's words, "By the word of the Lord the heavens were made" (Psalms 33:6). God speaks, and it is good. God communicates with creation through humankind. God initiates an everlasting covenant with words that promise, "I will make you exceedingly numerous" (Genesis 17:2b); "I will make of you a great nation" (Genesis 12:2a); "I will give to you, and to your offspring after you, the land where you are now an alien" (Genesis 17:8a). These are words that also require actions, signs of the covenant on the part of humankind. These are words that, according to God, should be kept in your heart, recited to your children and written on your doorposts (Deuteronomy 6:6–9).

The covenant is two-way. As God speaks to us, we speak to God. Christ is the logos incarnate. Word is sacramental, "a visible (or audible) sign of

God's invisible grace." Word as sacrament is a leap from God to us. In the same way, our human words, our language bridges the gaps between us. Words bridge the separation between us that requires communication. For Rev. Peggy Johnson and her deaf congregation that uses American Sign Language for communication, the Word of God must be enacted. It must be shown. "You can't just talk about it," she says, "Word must be flesh or it doesn't dwell."[4] Of course, words can also widen that gap, pull us apart. Despite that, we are called into the sacrament of conversation with God and each other. Yet in attempting to overcome that separation even temporarily, human communication has the potential of becoming sacramental, of bearing God between us—that is the impetus, our reason for preaching and teaching.

In her landmark work of 1989, *The Power to Speak: Feminism, Language, God,* Rebecca Chopp names feminist discourses of "emancipatory transformation" as proclamation of that Word of God.[5] In chapter three I situate back talk into the context of biblical and historical traditions in which holy conversation takes place. I believe that we continue to need back talk as part of our theological methodology within that covenantal relationship with God and each other. I believe that when women and men in our history have spoken out against injustice, they truly were standing on hallowed ground. Martin Luther King, Jr., Rosa Parks, and Oscar Romero did not just speak out. They *acted* out of their convictions. Though our speech may not be as eloquent or memorable as some of those named, when we ask for needed change, we are walking on holy ground. Though our words are ordinary and sometimes poorly chosen, our talk can be holy. Through our human words, God speaks. Holy talk is not just words, but words that call us to act.

Why do we need to talk back to the church? Does the church really need changing that badly? What is so bad, after all, about the church? First, let me affirm the church! It has spoken and continues to speak the message of the Gospel. There is a lot that is right with the church. It continues to do the work of bringing about God's vision in the world. Yet, having grown up in the church and served it in a variety of positions, having held just about every office in the church except organist, having taught in two seminaries, and having seen legions of my colleagues felled by the church's army of resistance, I have a deep sense that the church fails in its mission in many ways. As soon as we forget the mandate to be always reforming, we stop being the church. Interestingly, Roman Catholic educator Thomas Groome says that rather than considering only part of Christiandom as protesters (Protestants), the baptismal mandate of *all* Christians is to protest anything that is not of God's reign.[6]

To test this sense of needed change I have surveyed and interviewed men and women, lay and clergy in the U.S. I also talked with some women in the Church of England and in Korean churches in the U.S. and Korea. I talked with men and women who felt they were outside the mainstream. I also talked with clergy who have done well in their denominations, according to standards by which we usually measure, such as holding an upper-level position or pastoring a "large steeple church." I heard their stories of success and encouragement. However, they are not immune to struggle. I asked them what changes they have seen and how they think the church still needs to change. I asked them what one thing they would change about the church. I also asked them how women have helped to bring about change. I have found their responses to be quite illuminating.

This study is not a quantitative one. Instead, any time I went to conferences or local churches, I randomly invited church folks to answer my questionnaire or to talk with me. I also asked friends and acquaintances in ministry to ask parishioners to respond. In spite of our assumption that people resist change, 90 percent of those I surveyed or interviewed said that yes, the church needs to change. Because the changes they say are needed are numerous, I have categorized them into five distinct but related areas for change and growth. These are changes that women's leadership is bringing and may continue to bring to fruition, and they coalesce into a kind of vision, what Shirley Nelson called "a preposterous hope" of what the church can be.[7] In subsequent chapters I share my own thoughts and those of people I have interviewed as to how to bring about these changes. The changes that people are calling for in the church go further than holding the church accountable to be the church it should be. Yes, it is true that we ought to be more engaged in mission, less fragmented, and more ecumenical, that we ought to have a clear vision. There are a lot of "oughts" and "shoulds." The changes I have identified in my research are perhaps less grandiose and more earthy and practical. Some are the gut reactions of people who love and value the church but have found resistance to their leadership. I do not intend to languish in a "preachy" mode. Rather, talking with church leaders has inspired me, renewed my hope, and illuminated basic, gospel values in new ways for me that speak to how the church can be.

Honest Ways of Talking to Ourselves and to the World

Hands down this was the area of change most called for by those I surveyed and interviewed. People expressed this need in different ways, but it boiled down to truth telling. I find this to be a crucial revelation for the church today. It was almost uncanny that so many people voiced this needed change. Many said they were tired of the manipulation and deception they have seen in the church. One pastor confided: "Those on the margins, who come and sit in the pew and are not really involved may not notice it. But once you are in ministry it slaps you in the face. It is dishonesty of the hierarchy, deception by supposed colleagues. This ugly monster takes many forms."[8] This person renounced "all the passive-aggressive behavior in the church. It seems that the church is a haven for this sort of thing." "Dishonesty is a huge problem in the church. We cannot ignore it," another said.

The lack of honesty sometimes takes the form of backstabbing or competition or out-and-out lying. One woman left the ministry because another pastor on the staff of the church she served persisted in "badmouthing" her all over the church, criticizing every thing she did, her preaching, her teaching, her theology, even how she dressed. She asked to move to another church but did not receive a new appointment. Rather than face another year of such grief, she found something else to do. Some would say that her call was just not strong enough, that it was her own fault. That is what people say when they do not want to acknowledge their own complicity in someone's suffering. One would like to think that integrity wins out in the end, but in this case, the male pastor succeeded somehow in gaining support while she felt abandoned. Extremely disillusioned with the church and hurt by remarks that indicated she just couldn't hack it, this woman's scars run deep. She still feels called to the ministry and grieves every day that she is not pastoring.

Dishonesty can be a means of protecting the hierarchy. We have been pummeled by news reports on sexual abuse conducted by clerics in the Roman Catholic Church and the alleged cover-up by the hierarchy. Such things are not limited to the Roman Catholics, of course. To view this as a problem only in the Catholic Church ignores the broader implications for church leaders everywhere and from all traditions. We are not trusted! Churches and ministers that shelter sexual predators are abusers themselves by their own collusion in the act. My Roman Catholic friends are experiencing deep hurt because what affects the few affects the many. Perhaps the demand for more honesty reflects the media attention to the bad name that the church has earned in all this.

Sometimes the dishonesty takes the form of not telling someone the truth they need to hear simply because it is easier and more politically advantageous to keep quiet. The language of false consent, of keeping silent, or nodding approval to something we really don't agree with is pervasive, but back talk may be an antidote. The "Don't ask, Don't tell" policy of some denominations toward homosexuals in ministry is an example of the lack of honesty. Some denominations have legislation that prohibits the ordination of openly gay or lesbian persons. Episcopal priest Carter Heyward calls the church's expectation that gay people will and must lie about their lives an "ethic of flagrant duplicity."[9] If God has called a gay person into ministry, as long as that person keeps her or his sexuality a secret, he or she is allowed to serve and may be ordained. "It is living a lie," one woman told me. "The church tells me that if I lie, I can fulfill my call and will be okay. If I don't lie, I disobey God's call to me to go into ministry. Somewhere I remember that Christianity is supposed to promote truth telling. People are afraid to speak out against this because of jeopardizing their position in the hierarchy." Some recent challenges to this position in several denominations provide hope.

The church often postures itself as being unconditionally accepting, but it is not. What it often offers is merely pseudo-community, what Jürgen Moltmann called a Noah's Ark of isolated individuals.[10] We are seeing the rise of alternative churches as proof of this: gay and lesbian congregations, biker churches, trucker churches, women's churches, etc., as more and more people feel they do not fit the traditional mold and refuse to participate in the homogeneous churches of North America. One may understand the rationale for these alternative communities, but how far will this go?

Being honest means that sometimes we express anger. Yet anger has been forbidden to women, who are supposed to be nice and suppress it. Feminists have been accused and vilified for operating out of a hermeneutic of anger. Women's anger has more often than not been trivialized, invalidated, considered over-reacting, bitchy, or relabeled as PMS. Back talk could be deemed as angry talk. Anger, according to Beverly Wildung Harrison, provides the energy to take on the work or restoration and change. She says, "The power of anger is the work of love." Think of the well-known organization called MADD, Mothers Against Drunk Driving. These women took their personal pain and anger and put it to good use. Angry and rightfully so, they talked back to a legal system that looked the other way at drunk driving. I have become aware of Argentina's *Madres de Plaza de Mayos* (Mothers of the Disappeared) who, out of anger at the loss of children and family members, organize political rallies against violence. The anger of these and other groups of women is the work of love.[11] Chung Hyun-Kyung has pointed to the concept of *han* in feminist Asian theology. Han is anger or resentment, and it is necessary for making sense of their experience of suffering. For example, she names the suffering of the "comfort women" forced to sexually serve American soldiers during World War II.[12]

More women and men are holding the church accountable for telling the truth. Many of those I have talked with say we must uphold honesty and in so doing find more ways to heal conflict. John R. Matthews contends that the male approach to conflict as a contest that evokes the competitive use of power influenced the popular dictum in the '70s seminars that conflict cannot be resolved, but only managed. The implication is that conflict must be kept alive and controlled, that conflict is "an arena necessary to being masculine." In contrast, Matthews documented an approach to working with conflict in the church practiced by many women, which tries to draw people closer to one another and open the lines of communication so there might be healing.[13]

One woman wrote, "We have to call people to be Christ-like. We have a moral obligation as Christians to tell the truth, to love one another and to tell the truth."

Affirm Women's Leadership

Many say that we need to affirm and support women's leadership, especially that of black, Hispanic, African, and Asian women. Sixty-eight percent of the people I surveyed said something to this effect. The common sentiment was that we have not been doing this enough. Almost as many men as women named this need. One of my colleagues pointed out that this response may be skewed because some of the people I surveyed knew me and knew I was doing research on women in ministry, and were telling me what I wanted to hear. Still, I tend to take people at face value and assume enough people are calling for this kind of change to warrant taking a look at how we might bring about this change.

Women have made great strides in ministry but still struggle despite their proven competence as a group. Several studies confirm that women are leaving the ordained ministry at a higher rate than men.[14] Yes, more women are coming in, but we lose the gifts of those that give up and leave. There are far too many stories of the church not affirming and actively resisting women in ministry. Non-white women have twice the struggle, many still being denied ordination in their denomination. Some are not given clergy appointments because of their accents or color. Women have been rejected by their congregations simply because they were women *before* they even arrived to begin their ministry.

An African American laywoman who had expressed a call to ministry was told by a male pastor, "You can come up from the congregation to give the prayer. I don't want to sit with a woman in the chancel." A Chinese clergywoman was actually told by a chair of a staff-parish relations committee, "We don't want a woman here, much less an Oriental." It sounds far-fetched, but these are real stories. Are they the exception? Hopefully, but they should not happen at all. Some clergywomen tell me that they do not experience such prejudice and feel their ministry has always been affirmed, but acknowledge that this is not the case with many of their friends.

Other women have felt that their acceptance has been conditional. One woman said, "Women need to focus on leading the church rather than having to fight to be accepted as a minority." Many of the women I talked with say they dream of the day when their gender is not an issue. After preaching what she thought was a spirit-filled sermon, one student pastor said that all people could talk about was the fact that she had had her hair cut and that they liked her new hair style. Rosemary Ruether has named sexism as a sin that calls for a "radical redefinition" of ministry and church.[15] Until the day comes when women can just be in ministry without the added burden of being pioneers, gender differences are something we have to deal with in the church, according to one female pastor.

A pervasive problem is that while gender inequalities in leadership are real and significant, perceptions of inequalities are not. For example, some men and women are keenly aware of, have experienced or observed discrimination against women while others have never had a problem. Those who have not seen the inequalities firsthand sometimes narrowly assume they don't exist. Deborah L. Rhode cites the first female CEO of Hewlett Packard, who indicated at the time of her appointment that her accomplishment proves there is no glass ceiling. According to Rhode this view does not square with the facts. Though enormous progress has been made by women over the last several decades, one CEO does not balance the scale with the overrepresentation of women at the bottom of both the public and private sectors.[16]

To enter the debate on gender differences is to walk into a tornado. Questions about what it means to be female or male touch a nerve, according to linguist Deborah Tannen.[17] Are gender differences inborn? The result of socialization? Culturally imposed? The result of evolutionary survival? Little boys are often taught to be competitive and aggressive and to conquer. Little girls are conditioned to be, and reinforced for being, cooperative and sympathetic. Moreover, for the last twenty-five years there has been much debate about leadership and gender difference. Some of the debate focuses on the glass ceilings and bias against women. Some of it focuses on possible gender differences in style, priorities, and effectiveness. There is widespread agreement, according to Rhode, that gender does make a difference in "virtually all aspects of social experience," but little consensus on the nature and origins of those differences, or how those differences are experienced by different groups in different contexts.[18] Tannen suggests that the disagreement is based on methodology. Social scientists trained in scientific method may discount ethnographic research because it lacks large data samples or statistical analysis. Ethnographers may scorn social science research because it is based on data elicited in a controlled, laboratory environment and not in a natural setting. Ethnographic research leads more credence to the existence of gender differences.[19]

Because ministry was and continues to be in some ways a male-dominated profession, the practice of ministry reflected the acculturation of males. One thing in the past that worked against women is that stereotypical characteristics associated with women were not traditionally associated with leadership. The typical male clergy profile of twenty-five years ago was characterized by strong, aggressive leadership and decision making, by invulnerability and by a "lone-ranger mode of operating." The clergy who exhibited the most aggressiveness, ambition, and self-sufficiency were the most successful and rated the highest.[20]

In the past it has also been the consensus that if women act in certain ways, if they play by men's rules, they can go far. Kathy Bushkin, senior vice president for Corporate Relations and president of the AOL Time Warner Foundation, told about when she first started working in Washington, D.C., in 1972 as a press secretary. She relayed how she had to adapt to a man's world. "We learned to get along with the guys. We thought we had to, and it got exhausting." Now she has learned the importance of maintaining her own identity.[21]

Judy Rosener, a professor in the Graduate School of Management of the University of California Irvine, wrote: "In the 1970s, women succeeded the only way they could, by imitating the qualities and characteristics associated with their male colleagues.... [Now] they are succeeding because of, not in spite of, certain characteristics generally considered to be feminine and 'inappropriate'."[22]

Women have discovered, according to journalist Leslie Milk, that while it is helpful to learn the games their mothers never taught them and to dress for success, they do not have to follow conventional wisdom about the way people in power positions should think, act, or lead.[23] In ministry, the women who were the "ice-breakers" made their way by "beating men at their own game," according to John R. Matthews. In order to succeed they had to excel in the "ways of control, competitiveness and emotional invulnerability." These women made a great contribution, and it is largely due to these ice-breakers that women in ministry now have the opportunity to be themselves. Further, by being themselves, Matthews says, they may be changing the profession of ministry.[24]

Pastor Ruth Mellon shared another side to the problem. As long as she was meek and mild and nice, she was accepted. When she was perceived as trying to push her own ideas and not acquiescing to the strong male chair of the Staff-Parish Relations (SPR) committee, she angered him and several others and was accused of being a dictator. Carol Becker pointed to this trap in ministry. As long as a woman is feminine, attractive, and acts in ways that are acceptable, she is fine. If she tries to be herself, and that happens to be different from conventional understandings of femininity, she is a threat.

Becker told of one woman who was denied advancement because she was deemed too assertive. She felt that if she had been a male, her style would have been affirmed. She adopted a male style effectively, she thought, but was punished because as a woman, she was not supposed to be so aggressive.[25]

Importantly, Debra E. Meyerson from Stanford University's School of Education and Robin J. Ely, a professor at Harvard University School of Business Administration, caution that in celebrating femaleness we do not want to lock women into oppressive conventions of femininity or regulate women to performing only the housekeeping duties of an organization.[26] Socially sanctioned definitions of womanhood may confine and perpetuate what Rebecca Chopp calls the social-symbolic order, a pattern of values established by the dominant group. She critiques what she calls the feminism of "romantic expressivism," which romanticizes the differences between women and men and praises the so-called feminine qualities such as nurturing, warmth, and relationship building. She claims these "gifts" are assigned to women by present forms of patriarchy.[27] But to me this says women are passive victims incapable of resisting patriarchal stereotyping, and we are beyond that. I think Chopp is correct in that not all women are the same, of course. They do not all possess the same gifts. We need to move beyond false universalizing and essentialism. We are *more* than our gender.

Chopp applauds difference and the need for multiplicity, creativity, and affirmation of different voices. If a woman is nurturing and noncompetitive and feels comfortable with that style, why should she change it to adapt to the male model or abandon it in the name of feminism? Back talk is an act of defiance, an act of freedom to reject prescribed ways of being. Women still struggle to define their leadership, and they are increasingly finding its acceptance.

Whereas Rosemary Ruether has written that to acknowledge gender differences is to accept a hierarchy in which men dominate, other feminists such as Sara Butler argue that differences do not necessarily imply hierarchical relations.[28] She explores a theological anthropology that affirms "two ways of being body, two incarnations." Her view sees sexual difference as a value, "an image of the trinity," and does not see women and men as mutually antagonistic. To say that there are no differences in men and women leads to the notion that everybody is the same, and the "same" usually is defined by white male standards. In acknowledging differences, it does not necessarily follow that females or males are only suitable for certain roles. Rosemary Ruether does acknowledge that men and women have different experiences. Perhaps they just bring different things to the role. I like what Carter Heyward has written: "Our transforming power is not inherent to our gender....Our power lies in our having been born, nurtured, and acculturated into a corporate symbol: a symbol not necessarily of 'femininity,' but rather a symbol of difference."[29]

The double bind that women face relates to their language as well. In a well-known 1975 work, *Language and Women's Place,* Robin Lakoff says that women in certain cultures are trained to speak like "ladies," which causes men to perceive them as weak. Yet if they do adopt the language patterns of men and male ways of communicating, then they are seen as pushy and domineering. Linguistic style is developed through socialization and is especially noticeable between genders. Little boys are rewarded by their peers for talking up their achievements, whereas little girls are rewarded for playing theirs down. Lakoff and others found that women use provisional speech, tag questions ("It's hot, isn't it?"), qualifiers, and hedgers more than men, and these give them the appearance of being apologetic or unsure.[30] Some ways of talk are associated with women as a class, not as individuals. The context is important as well—not just what we say but how and where we say it. In a comparative study of men and women preachers, Catherine Ziel identified differences in the syntax used by women and men and tested the effects on their hearers. She found that the women preachers used almost twice as many qualifiers and hedgers as men and that women tended to use more socially inclusive speech in their preaching, such as preferring to use "we" rather than "you." They also used more verbs related to feeling ("I feel" or "we hope"). Ziel concluded that women preachers are more likely to "identify with their hearers and to include themselves among those addressed." Ziel asked congregants to listen to sermons preached by women and men and evaluate them. Interestingly, the congregants found women's preaching to be just as convincing and authoritative as the men's.[31]

In certain settings, though, women's authority is not recognized or may be tested. Women know all too well the experience of saying something in a meeting that is ignored until a man says the same thing, and it is suddenly the best idea since sliced bread. The consequences of differences in linguistic style tends to work against members of groups who are marginalized and stigmatized in our society and to the advantage of those in power, according to Tannen. In U.S. businesses, for example, where men's speaking style still dominates, women may be ignored, interrupted, and passed over for promotions, even if they are highly competent.[32]

To admit gender difference is not to deny that dominance exists. On the contrary, dominance is constructed by differences and not due to essential male or female traits. Dominant powers have used differences to construct and reinforce patterns of dominance—that is why many feminists have attempted to deny differences—so "difference" cannot be used against us. Tannen believes that we must move beyond the difference/dominance debate.[33] Lakoff's and Tannen's work has been criticized by some, and Tannen has been misunderstood and regulated to the "two cultures theory" such as espoused in *Men are from Mars, Women Are From Venus.* She has been accused of saying that when men and women misunderstand each other, no one is at fault—for example, in date rape. Tannen denies that her work implies this, and she supports efforts against domination.

We can use differences to counter domination and subjugation. To affirm women's leadership means that we overcome that double bind, and back talk is a way of communicating that attempts to do that. It does not require women to rid their speech of syntax that they are comfortable with, but is a form of communication that invites others into dialogue. Back talk creates open space and gives others permission to agree or disagree. Back talk is used to establish connection while at the same time challenging some sacrosanct preconceptions. Rather than being suspicious or afraid of another opinion, back talk welcomes it and relishes the opportunity to think together.

Writer Madeleine L'Engle echoes this need to affirm women's leadership. She writes that despite the literal presence of women, we still are waiting for the feminine to fully emerge in the church: "What I want ordained women to do is to be women, to bring the female part of the human being back into the church. The masculine part is already there, and I do not want to dispose of it." [34] Affirmation of women's leadership needs to come not only from the church and from their male colleagues, it has to come from other women. In *The Web of Women's Leadership,* Jacqulyn Thorpe and I talk about the women-against-women syndrome in ministry. More descriptions of this have cropped up, and we have become aware of more insights into this phenomenon. Jane Goodall shocked people in the 1960s with her finding that some female chimps kill the young of other females in an effort to maintain their dominant position in the colony. Why should we be so self-righteously shocked when we humans do it, too, if not literally, certainly figuratively speaking?

Deborah Tannen attributes women's poor treatment of each other to the fact that girls and women struggle to be included in community. In fact, community is so important to them that they struggle to be included in it every bit as much as boys and men struggle for status and power. When they fear exclusion, women might resort to most any means to avoid it.[35] Phyllis Chesler, in her controversial book *Woman's Inhumanity to Woman,* refers to the "shadow side" of female relationships.

Although second-wave feminists have assumed that sisterhood and solidarity is powerful and society has had to redefine gender roles and relations, still any gains of women have been hampered by a "rarely acknowledged reality" that women often betray other women. Whereas feminists are supposed to support one another and be in solidarity, there is still the "don't trust other women, they are your worst enemy" sentiment. We would like the loyalty of the Ya-Ya sisterhood but sometimes feel betrayed by other women. Chesler has been researching and writing about this for twenty-plus years, what she calls the "hard, mean world of post-feminist competition." She says that women are socialized as well as men to hold sexist ideas, and women are not just victims, but victimizers as well. Although men are more prone to physical violence, according to some studies, women may use indirect aggression such as shunning or malicious gossip. The sexism of women can be harder to identify and resist because it very often occurs behind the scenes.[36]

Delores C. Carpenter, however, points out that because it is men who still control the church, it is men and not women who are keeping women out, and she refutes the notion that it is mostly women who oppose women.[37] Resistance from women does exist, as many of the women I interviewed relayed. Perhaps because we expect and desire solidarity and support from other women, when this does not happen, their opposition becomes most noticeable and hurtful. Linda Hollies says that women have been "kept on the other side of the Old Boy's Club walls so long that now we find ourselves better than they are at erecting them against each other."[38]

Judith Briles, a corporate consultant, surveyed hundreds of business executives. Sixty-five percent of those reported that they had been treated unethically by a man and 47 percent reported unethical treatment by a woman. There may be fewer women in a position to treat anyone unethically, but the survey revealed that women were more likely to behave unethically to other women than to men. Briles found that women did not act unethically to get ahead as men did; rather, women did so because they were jealous or afraid someone was after their job. In one case she discussed, a female superior had several talented female subordinates fired and one even jailed because this supervisor was sure there was a coup in the works.[39] Women's resistance to each other will only diminish women's effectiveness in the church.

For those who have experienced this struggle and shared this pain, however, we cannot be content to sit back and do nothing. We have to talk back to the rejection. When one suffers, we all suffer. I believe that we can more fully affirm and recognize the blessing of women's leadership in ministry.

New Organization/Open Structure

Another need for change that was often named was the need for alternative ways of being and doing church. Many expressed frustration with common church structures that are not working anymore. "The current, denominationally driven structure is not fostering lay leadership. It is either burning people out or not attracting people to serve," said one survey participant. Ironically, though there is great spiritual hunger among the public, there is also a good deal of institutional alienation. What does it mean to be institutionally alienated? For one thing, it may mean that people are less interested in contributing their time and money to keep an institution going. Popular author Phillip Yancey has written a book on people "whose faith survived the church" *(Soul Survivor: How My Faith Survived the Church)*. Funny that we think of church as something one has to survive. He is correct that alienation from the church and bad experiences with church are a universal phenomenon. Have we become what Madeleine L'Engle calls "a thin and humorless church" where it is difficult to grow spiritually within its confines?[40]

What does attract people to the church is the Good News of the gospel message in an unpredictable world. The sureness of God's promise still calls people as it always has. The joy of celebration of life and goodness that combats evil, and the worship of this power of love beyond ourselves are the kinds of things that will bring people to the Christian faith and to the church. Of course, we may have to constantly change and adapt our language and ways of talking to the culture, but God is still attractive. People still fall in love with God every day. They want, they desire to adore and learn more about that God and to do so with others. Human beings are basically social animals. Although there is evidence that we have retreated more into ourselves in the last decade, humans still are a species that seek to belong, that live in groups, in ever-widening social circles. So people want to practice their faith and share its joy with others. The idea of Christian community, of koinonia, is very much alive and well. Yet the Christian community that exists as committees is increasingly not attracting people.

Now, structure is a good thing. We need structure, and it should be our friend! Boundaries help to organize us and to guide our efforts to make us effective for God's work. There are some hopeful models emerging for new organization. In *The Web of Inclusion,* Sally Helgesen addresses some of those and the headway that connectional leadership styles are making in business toward fostering a user-friendly structure. While this book does not propose one particular new structure for the church, I did get some ideas from talking with people about what is working.

I was very impressed and inspired when I visited the Ghana Wesleyan Methodist Church in Arlington, Virginia. Only six months old, this congregation of 70–100 members practices their Christian faith in the British Methodist tradition of their homeland. I was curious about their structure and how they operated, so I talked with them and observed them in action. They do not yet have a pastor and are in the process of discerning their identity and if they can affiliate with The United Methodist Church. They carry out intergenerational worship, education, and missions in a uniquely African way of "circle" decision making. Before or after a worship and fellowship on Sunday or Friday evenings, they meet in a circle and talk about the issue at hand. Everyone has a say. They are a most respectful and humble people, careful not to rush their decision making and concerned that each person feels heard. They do not always agree with one another. They care for the sick and those in need among them. I asked if they had committees for different things they do and was told that was not the way they work. People just volunteer for different responsibilities as they are moved to do so and as they are gifted.

I heard about Rachel Lewis, a clergywoman who had great success with a new form of organization in her local church (or new for her denomination). She enthusiastically talked with me about it. Rachel told me how she began with worship by trying some new things. The people seemed to respond to her. She started to hold regular gatherings at her house for prayer.

> When I first came to this church there was so much conflict and territorialism. I knew I was in for a rough ride. After I had been there for a few months, I met with the Administrative Council and suggested that I turn one room in the church into a ministry room where folks could gather and work. They were skeptical at first, but agreed to give it a shot.

The ministry room, Rachel says, is where she hangs out during the week.

> I have an office with sofas and chairs for counseling, and one at home if I need some space to do concentrated work, but my style is to work with the people. The ministry room is where everything happens. When I am at the church, I am in there talking with people, sharing ideas. I also spend time visiting and working in the community. I'm active in a community youth worship. I try to model what lay people can do. I gave up trying to get people to serve on committees that they didn't know the purpose of anyway. Now the Administrative Council meets on Sunday evening for supper and we talk about where we think the Spirit is leading us. The council is about twenty-five people. Others come and bring their ideas as well. I have no trouble getting people to be on the council. They clamor to be on it because it is exciting. It is just one meeting and it really isn't a meeting; it is really a discernment or listening. Some people call this conferencing. Maybe that's it.

Rachel told me how people on the Council then mobilize other people to help with whatever needs to be done. She explained how this was different from the usual process of a large group handing something over to a committee to implement and then abandoning it. Often what happens in that case, she said, was an idea falls through the cracks. In her church two or three people are moved and then galvanize others to be involved. Her role as pastor is to support, guide, give advice, and offer resources.

> It all takes place within the larger context of the community so you do not have a lot of "lone guns" running around stepping on each other. Some peo-

ple also participate in small group Bible study, prayer and support groups. Several people organize Sunday school. They get together and work in the ministry room. When someone wants to try something new they bring it to the council and usually the council gives its blessing. I've quit hearing, "We've never done it that way before." We are known as a church open to new ideas, but one that is spiritually centered. We have also very little territorialism anymore. They used to say "That's my file cabinet, don't touch it" or "That's the education desk, don't put your stuff there." Now, in the ministry room, it's share and share alike. Everybody works on everything. We have two wonderful administrative assistants who keep things in order and labeled, so it is not chaos. The best thing is that people do not feel overwhelmed with work and responsibility with little appreciation.[41]

Harrison Owen is well known for promoting what he calls Open Space Technology (OST). While primarily used in business and other organizations, it has, I believe, implications for the church. He described a meeting that took place in 1992 for the purpose of deciding the expenditure of $1.5 billion designated for highway construction on tribal and public lands. The people that gathered for the meeting, Native Americans, government officials, and state and local politicians, all had a stake in how the money was to be spent. The participants were historically divided on many issues. It had the potential, he claimed, of being another unproductive and conflicted meeting. When the participants arrived, however, there was no advanced agenda. Everyone knew when the meeting was to begin and end and that there was a task before them. When they gathered, they were surprised to find a room with two large circles of chairs with nothing in the middle and a large blank wall on one side of the room. Each person was invited to post a sheet of newsprint identifying a topic of conversation and to name a time for that conversation to take place. Anyone who wanted to join in that conversation arrived at the designated place and time. After the conversations had been held, the whole group met to formulate a plan. Information was fed into a computer and a report generated. The level of synergy and excitement in the room quickly led them to action. Many commented on the fact that everyone had a voice in the proceedings and felt good about decisions they made. Owen believes that overplanning, control, and fragmentation may lessen the productivity of a group. Yet, he warns, OST is not for every group or situation:

In the wrong situation OST may create more problems than it solves. Open Space Technology is effective in situations where a diverse group of people must deal with complex and potentially conflicting material in innovative and productive ways. It is particularly powerful when nobody knows the answer and the ongoing participation of a number of people is required to deal with the questions. Conversely, Open Space Technology will not work, and therefore should not be used, in any situation where the answer is already known, where somebody at a high level *thinks* he or she knows the answer, or where that somebody is the sort that *must* know the answer, and therefore must always be in charge, otherwise known as control, control, control. [42]

For my money, the church is an organization that is diverse and must deal with complex material in a changing environment, and that no one person has all the right answers. However, some do think of the church as a place where one or two provide the answers, and some church leaders see themselves in that role. So the Catch-22 is that we may need something like OST, but we might not be ready for it. A church in Illinois and its pastoral leadership finds itself at odds with denominational hierarchy because the church moved to a structure that differs from what was mandated, but that worked better for this congregation. Sometimes conventional structure, however, is less imposed, than simply accepted because that's the way it's always been done or because of a lack of understanding or consideration of alternative approaches.

I believe that a connectional system of the church is not for the purpose of dictating the agenda, strategies, and structure of the church, but for the purpose of guiding, creating unity in diversity, teaching, and being prophetic. There is a huge difference in these two understandings. A connectional church is united in tradition, open to diversity, and also one that extends to the margins and brings people together in the love of Christ to serve the world.

Understanding the connectional church primarily as a system of institutional governance rather than as a union for ministry ignores the fact that each congregation has a unique call to ministry, a call very much determined by the congregation's location and context and by the gifts, resources, and needs of the church and community.

Ministry is no longer a matter of doing what we know how to do best. Nor is it adequate for congregations to continue to do what they did last year. The time and environment continue to change at a pace that requires us constantly to evaluate, to learn anew what our purpose of ministry is, and continually to reinvent the congregation to meet the needs that face us.[43]

The changes demand new forms of congregational life and ministry. We can affirm a connectional way of being the church without imposing old, worn-out structures. We are no longer, if we ever were, a "one-size-fits-all" church.

New Lay Leadership

Closely related to the need for alternative structures is the need for lay leadership and new kinds of lay leadership. The emphasis on lay leadership in renewal movements in the church flies in the face of traditional clericalism. Women, according to Troxell and Farris and other sources, are more inclined to treat laity as equals and to inspire lay leadership.[44]

A committee structure common in many churches often takes a programmatic approach to ministry that many of the church leadership books say is waning rapidly. For example, a mission committee of six people worked hard for one full year to plan a mission festival. They labored under the leadership of a dedicated, if hard to get along with, chairperson who cracked the whip to make sure people did what they were supposed to do. The purpose of the festival was to let people know what was going on in missions and to encourage more people to get involved in them. Several thousands of dollars were spent bringing in speakers and entertainers, on publicity and food, supplies, etc. The event day came and only fifteen people came other that those invited to display and those who provided the leadership. One could argue that fifteen people is fifteen people and that, as I've said myself, numbers are not important. More significant perhaps was the fact that there was no noticeable increase in the interest or involvement in missions in that congregation. This is not to be negative, just realistic. But a year's worth of work for so little an impact is not only discouraging, it signals that we are doing something wrong.

I am convinced that programming is no longer what people need or want from the church. In the '60s, '70s, and '80s, programming was what defined the successful and growing church. What many of the people that I talked with want is relationship (with God and others); acceptance; challenging teaching and preaching; resources for living and making meaning. They want to get that through worship, serving others, one-on-one relationships, and Bible study.

The church, in a sense, has always had programs of some type. The forms of ministry described in Acts of *didache, diakonia, koinonia, kerygma,* and *leiturgia* indicate a kind of programming structure. There was the catechumenate, an elaborate program for initiating new converts and preparing them for baptism. Cultural conditions have at various times required church programming of a certain nature. The successful programmatic churches of the twentieth century were often led by the CEO male pastor overseer, while the programming and administration for the church came to be assigned to poorly paid, highly trained (in some cases) professionals. The demand for programs meant that churches needed to pay professionals to carry them out effectively. The professional paradigm for ministry perhaps had the side-effect of diminishing the laity's sense of ministry or of being needed. As a professional in ministry, I have struggled with that legacy and wondered if I was usurping the role of committed lay people. The church got into the habit of paying people (even if very little) to be in ministry. Now it is more difficult to find people even to pay.

While there is a long history of programming in the church, it seems that the programming model for ministry was taken to its extremes and reached its limits. Programming was often done *for* people, which contributed to and conditioned their passivity. In *The Godbearing Life: The Art of Soul Tending for Youth Ministry,* Kenda Creasy Dean and Ron Foster present a helpful contrast to a programming model of ministry with a mission model of ministry, and it is not just a shift for clergy, but for lay leadership as well.[45] Programming means lots of administration, and that is another one of the areas of change people are calling for—less administration.

Emerging models of ministry come out of an interest in spirituality and a desire for spiritual growth. These models of ministry seek to do more of their work through interpersonal relationships and collegiality rather than administratively, which is one definitive change that some women say they bring to the ministry. One church is organized around a cadre of lay ministers who have special training in certain ministries. Another has implemented an idea to establish lay ministry orders in which a group of laity form a community that gathers often and works together. Each community stays together for two years, and then new communities are formed.

Some seminaries have been innovative in inviting lay people into theological education and are no longer seen just as schools for preachers.

Biblical and Theological Reflection

In keeping with the turn to spirituality and lay leadership, many are calling for fresh opportunities for biblical and theological reflection. People I interviewed expressed this as a need for spiritual growth and Christian formation, as a turn away from shallow, half-hearted, and rote participation to a genuine struggle for faith in the context of community. The sense is that the seminary-trained pastor is no longer the one holding the answer sheet. As an educator I resonate with this felt need but question where and when this would take place. Offering more classes seems fruitless when lives are already so busy. Pastors and educators lament the biblical illiteracy in their congregations and tell me their parishioners are uncomfortable about their knowledge of the Bible. Yet at the same time there is a growing curiosity and willingness to sit down with others and study.

Sally Simmel addressed the question of why lay people would want to engage in theological reflection and education in the book, *A Lifelong Call to Learn: Approaches to Continuing Education for Church Leaders,* edited by Robert E. Reber and D. Bruce Roberts. We live in a world that has been described as permanent whitewater. "In a complex and changing world where chaos and tragedy are always within a hair's breath, where our towers of meaning come crashing down both literally and metaphorically, people face the difficult task of finding meaning and interpreting the faith. An understanding of vocation helps answer that question. The church teaches that God calls all Christians by virtue of their baptism."[46] Christian vocation is the response a person makes to the address of God to use our gifts to bring about God's vision for the world. We who are called are expected to show in our daily life and work that we are called. The divine call is the call to conversion, to a life of faith and a call to live out that faith in a particular way. Theological reflection is one way that people can figure out how to live out their faith to be leaders in the faith community, whether out front or behind the scenes, and to bear witness to the Kin-dom of God. Biblical and theological reflection will involve a partnership between seminaries and churches and will take place in both. Getting laity into the seminary and providing them access to theological education will give laity a better understanding of ministry as well as the theological basis for it. It will offer those preparing for professional ministry a sense of what lay people are facing in the world and how clergy and laity can work as partners to bring the message of the church in the world. Most clergy, I believe, would welcome this partnership.

Yet accomplishing this atmosphere of theological reflection will take some back talk. Back talk will be needed to dispel some assumptions about how and where theological reflection can take place. There is some fear and trembling about lay people going to seminary. Seminaries often have the reputation of robbing good Christian men and women of their faith. While it is true that seminaries challenge assumptions or even rattle the foundations of faith, it is absurd to withhold theological education from lay people on the grounds that they cannot handle it. Clergy sometimes fear that if lay people knew what was *really* being taught in the seminaries, they would leave the church. Are not lay people entitled to the same information as clergy? Not only can they handle it, they relish it. My experience of twenty-plus years in the ministry tells me that lay people want to wrestle with theological issues, and they are interested in building practical skills. Some may have their faith rattled, some even may leave, but most will come to a deeper faith in which they will act to build up the Body of Christ and further the mission of the church in the world. I would add that while the laity stand to gain much from the seminary, the seminary stands to be greatly enhanced by the presence of lay students. We learn a lot from lay people, the challenges they face in the world, and they hold us accountable to our commitment to the church and to our mission.[47]

Theological reflection is, of course, not limited to the seminaries. Teresa Combith told me in an interview that her congregation is mostly elderly people who cannot come out at night. She engages them in "talk back" sessions during and after her sermons on Sunday. They now are more involved and responsive. "They pay attention more," she says, "and so do I."

Some have told me that they have grown and learned more in our "sessions" than in their entire fifty years as a church member. We talk together about questions and concerns that are real to them, like how to live with joy in the last years of their lives. We find meaning and insight in the Bible and we reflect on what God is saying to us.

Again, such reflection is not busy work. It takes place in what we *already do,* but perhaps what we do is more intentionally devoted to providing opportunity for growth. It takes place as we practice our faith, in the classic Christian practices of worship, study, conferencing, prayer, singing, fellowship, and mission. We engage in these Christian practices not to prove how Christian we are or to earn God's love or to achieve a star in our crown. The early reformers called that works righteousness—or being saved by works, the things we do. Works righteousness has the tone of "Jesus is coming, look busy." Martin Luther, as a monk, called this "monkery." Fewer people are tempted by works righteousness because they realize it is never enough. Christian practices are something we are led to do in response to God's love, out of our faith. Through these practices we are able to do what John Ackerman says in his book, *Listening to God: Spiritual Formation in Congregations,* is the task for every Christian community, which is simply to listen. Spiritual growth comes through really listening to God and attending to what God is doing right now. It is, in the words of Matthew 6:33, seeking first the kingdom of God.[48]

Like Ackerman, I am not big on spiritual fads. Often these really are ancient spiritual disciplines that are rediscovered and are helpful to people seeking a more meaningful faith. If these are helpful, then people should continue to do them, but not expect them to be a quick fix. One lay person I interviewed remarked:

> I believe that the church would be a different church altogether, that the world would be different if the church would lead us in a quest to find God. Sometimes we think we are doing that, but really we are too busy with all the "churchy" things we do. If we really sought ways of meeting God and discovered that God is interested in us, that God loves us and doesn't leave us alone, then I think that we would never be the same.

This quest is a lifelong process. I heard some interesting stories of how this is happening, which I share later in this book. I found a commitment from women leaders to lead the quest.

Shirley Nelson compared seeking change in the church to prospecting for gold. Once in a while you find a mother lode:

> These are not perfect churches, but they represent possibilities, and that is what we share. The odds are not what matters. We try and fail again, slowly

learning what it means to believe and to live the gospel. Where else but in the church of Christ can we practice what the world can't comprehend—the "nonsense" of the Prodigal Son, the Widow's Mite, the Good Samaritan, and the notion of losing our lives to find them. Where else can we explore the intricacies of applying that law of love, without silliness and naivete, until, to paraphrase Reinhold Niebuhr, the law of love becomes the ultimate measure of justice throughout the world.[49]

I am most thoroughly convinced that the church has a chance. I believe this primarily because I look for and see daily how God still calls people and still transforms them and still speaks to them in the deepest core of their being. I believe that when we speak honestly to ourselves and the world we gain credibility. We can stop trying to both fight against culture and stop being overtaken by it. We will be more than a warm and fuzzy place for weddings and funerals; we will actually be integral in people's lives, transforming people and the world around us. I have always had an activist bent and want the church to get out there and kick butt, so to speak, to make the world a better place. (Can you hear "Kum-ba-yah" yet?) I have had to learn to temper that rather self-righteous (works righteousness) drivel with some wisdom learned along the way. If the church is honest and lives out its testimony to the world, in the world, then the law of love will prevail.

• 3 •

NOT JUST TALKING HEADS
Biblical and Historical Perspectives on Back Talk!

WE STAND IN A LONG HISTORY AND ABIDE within proven traditions of those who have talked back for fundamental change. Back talk is not a new weapon for feminists to assert their wills and procure demands. Understanding leadership and the struggle for change is not simply a matter of an archeological dig, sifting through our experience for clues. Experience is a resource that we bring to the table, but not the only one that Christians bring. Early feminist theology contended that women's experience is authoritative for doing theology, and we cannot buy into faith that is contradictory toward or unconcerned with women's lives. The post-feminist predicament of Christian women with varying experiences has been to see themselves and place themselves in a largely patriarchally conceived tradition. Most of the women I interviewed attempted to integrate their experience into the framework of theology, scripture, and tradition, seeking to genuinely understand and appropriate their faith tradition from their particular place. Critics accuse feminist and liberation theologians of rewriting "The Tradition" to suit their own purposes. While some scholars do consider themselves to be revisionist thinkers, my contention is that we do not have to rewrite because we do not have one Christian tradition but many. Why should we assume that the white European male tradition is normative? We each bring our whole selves, our experience, our theological understandings, our faith history, our cultures, and our biases to the task of carving out a way of being in ministry. How we ought to be and live and do ministry is not just dictated externally. That would be too easy. Neither is it just a matter of "what works for me." New approaches to leadership in ministry come from many sources that we approach both critically and reverently.

Biblical Authority

The Bible is a troublesome part of the body of Christian traditions for feminists and, for that matter, many postmodern Christians. Its treatment of women, Jews, children, homosexuals, war, and divorce strike many as hopelessly outdated and unredeemable, if not just plain wrong. The problem is not only poor interpretation or bad hermeneutics (although that is a contributing factor), but stumbling blocks exist within the texts themselves. For many, rather than dispensing good news, the Bible is perceived as impossible to rescue from its patriarchal and hierarchical system.[1]

Critiquing the Bible is not new. Consider Marcion and Luther, and in the nineteenth century, Elizabeth Cady Stanton, Sojourner Truth, and Anna Julia Cooper, editors of *The Women's Bible,* and the challenges that the rise of historical-critical method presented.[2] The Bible arose from an androcentric culture with a patriarchal system of values. The Bible was written by men and canonized by men with an intentional effort to perpetuate the status quo. Is the Bible only for those of who can accept this system? Does it belong only to those who still claim its literalness and inerrancy? I do not believe so.

Many persons, despite the difficulty in justifying the claims of the Bible in today's world, still view the Bible as sacred scripture and still find spiritual nourishment from it. How can this be? Is it merely sentimental attachment? Again, I do not think so, or at least I hope not. Do we pick and choose which stories and passages that we will consider to be the Word of God for us, rejecting that which offends? Many preachers today do this. As Rosemary Ruether points out, this practice is not out of the question nor is it a new approach. Much of the Hebrew ritual laws and practices were abandoned, though these texts, of course, still appear in the canon.[3] Do we attempt hermeneutical legerdemain to salvage these acceptable parts? There is an increasing number of books on women of the Bible that seek more liberating interpretations of their roles. While I applaud their efforts and often find their insights helpful, I still find this answer to be inadequate. One cannot change the fact that women were regarded not as humans, but as property.

There is an important group of feminists who refuse to abandon the authority of the Bible in favor of experience, who seek to identify its enduring theological meaning and values. Another solution is posed by

Elizabeth Schüssler Fiorenza, which is to view the Bible not as an archetype, but as a historical prototype—a resource to utilize rather than an authority to follow. As a prototype, the Bible is abated, amplified, and developed by further revelation.[4] Yet it is not an either/or position, as we hold both views in tension.

Loraine MacKenzie Shepherd offers an important insight: "For a feminist theological method to be operative within a particular community, it must be accountable, in part, to the canonical system of that community."[5] Feminist interpretation may do this, she attests, by drawing connections between the "community's historical traditions and faith practices" and experience. Without some accountability, she judges, a feminist methodology could discount important sources of revelation found in the traditions and therefore could be too easily dismissed by the community.[6]

The question is not whether more of the Bible is in favor of justice and liberation than is not, or what parts are redeemable, but how we can read and understand the Bible for enduring theological value in today's faith communities. Often people are taught to read the Bible to find answers to their own dilemmas or struggles or to validate their opinions and practices. If one becomes cognizant of the faults of this hermeneutic, one struggles to ascertain the Bible's purpose. If the Bible is to tell us what to do and think, how can we justify its inconsistencies and our own conscience telling us that some of the biblical notions are not quite right? If the Bible isn't for this purpose, then what is it for? The Bible is for calling us to God, for calling us to task, shaking us up, and ultimately for "gospeling" us, bringing us into the good news of an earth-shattering love.

I believe that women's experience of oppression cannot be denied, but the biblical values plus that experience can co-exist. Rather than reject biblical authority outright, I find back talk a workable hermeneutic. The Bible is a very human book; therefore, we talk back to it. This is, of course, the premise of biblical criticism. In fact, the Bible begs to be talked back to. Theologian Kwok Pui-lan suggests that we see the Bible as a "talking book," a term she borrows from Henry Louis Gates in describing African American literature. Gates revealed how African Americans used the same books as their white masters but changed or subverted their messages and practices. In the same vein, Kwok refers to the Bible as a talking book in order to call for that subversive and imaginative reading by colonized people. The Bible as a talking book shifts the authority away from the literal text to the interpretive community and emphasizes its dialogic nature.[7]

Talking back is how we yield a healthy and hopeful experience with the Bible, how we can value its place among the Christian traditions and see it as part of a bigger picture. We need a way to argue with the text in love, as one might argue or dialogue with a spouse or a friend. When we do this, Bible study truly becomes a revolutionary activity. The following attempts to locate the method of back talk within the message as a means of both illuminating our biblical understanding as well as demonstrating how the method has served and contributed, even when it may not have been entirely successful. Following the recent work of several scholars, I relate back talk or sass to what may more precisely be called chutzpa (or *hutzpah* in the biblical tradition).

Chutzpa in the Bible

Precedent for talking back to the Bible comes from the Bible itself. Some scholars note that the Bible is, in fact, a talking back to God. "Holy chutzpa" is well known in the Jewish tradition. It is a very human attitude, simultaneously foolish and courageous, in which people talk back to God. Yiddish humor defines chutzpa as the case of the grandmother who accompanied her grandson to the beach. When a tidal wave washed her grandson out to sea, she cried out to God, "Please save him. I'll do anything." Another wave deposited her grandson at her feet. She looked heavenward and exclaimed, "He had a hat, you know!" Although chutzpa has a lighthearted side, it also has a weightier meaning in the Talmudic tradition. Rabbi Baruch HaLevi describes it as the willingness to act on our beliefs.[8] It is a dialectic of trust and questioning. In Judaism covenant is understood as a dialogue between a human and God, a two-way street.[9] According to one writer, chutzpa is a symbol for the human capacity to affect God. By the same token, the tradition that calls God into question also calls human beings into question.[10]

Belden C. Lane describes the Jewish tradition of arguing with God of "boldness with regard to heaven." Its long and continuous history is associated with the prophets and does not indicate disbelief, but a robust faith. Lane calls this *hutzpa k'lapei shamaya,* a unique form of prayer that "offers access to God's inner life."[11] This audaciousness comes from the human experience of suffering and adversity, and it "opens onto a landscape where

God and human beings walk as friends." Back talk, arguing with God, binds us to God even as it accuses God. This experience is absent in much of Christian spirituality, according to Lane, because it is not nice to talk back to God. Instead "placid devotion" prevails—an unquestioning faith that is spiritually and morally bankrupt.[12]

True biblical faith "limps like Jacob" from wrestling with God. Lane raises the question of how far one goes in speaking forcefully to God. Psalm 44 goes pretty far. The psalmist tells God to wake up:

> Rouse yourself! Why do you
> sleep, O Lord?
> Awake, do not cast us off
> forever!
> Why do you hide your face? Why do you forget our
> affliction and oppression? (Psalms 44:23–24)

Extreme situations provoke such language, such forceful, daring prayer.[13] The rabbis knew of the risks, however, and the wounds that might result. It was not to be used lightly nor in common liturgical settings. Though some called it blasphemy, others recognized that such talk brings one into the deepest encounter with God.

We are taught not to question God. Samuel Balentine expresses his personal experience with prayer:

> The church taught me how to pray and more subtly, how not to pray. One was to praise God, but not protest; to petition God, but not interrogate; and in all things accept and submit to the sometimes incomprehensible will of God, never challenge or rebel. Yet when life's circumstances would not permit either such passivity or such piety, this advocacy of a rather monotonic relation to God seemed destined to silence if not exclude me.[14]

Further he claims that the Bible does not support the portrait of a God that one is not allowed to question, petition, doubt, or even demand the "reversal of divine intentions." God's relation to humanity is firmly established, and the divine-human relationship is "fundamentally dialogical." The covenantal relationship, like human relationships, requires communication, and God engages humanity in a reciprocal relationship.[15]

So the Bible, even antiquated and frustrating, still calls us to listen to it, to hear its word proclaimed, still speaks to our souls. For in the Bible *all kinds of chutzpa is going on:* people arguing with God, singing while in exile, dry bones dancing, daughters prophesying, unclean people reaching for the Christ.[16] How about Abraham, who has the chutzpa to question God about the fate of Sodom and Gomorrah? "Shall not the Judge of all the earth do what is just?" (Genesis 18:25).[17] Jacob is, of course, the famed Godwrestler. God even declared Jacob (Israel) the winner, yet it was not without cost as he comes away with a limp.

Consider the story of Tamar, told in Genesis 38—a dicey one for many churchgoers. Though Tamar engages in deception and manipulative sex, one might admire her for taking matters into her own hands. Tamar is the daughter-in-law of Judah, the wife of his son Er. The Torah says that Er was wicked and God put him to death. To fulfill the obligations of levirate marriage, Tamar is given to Er's brother Onan so she might produce an heir for her dead husband. But Onan, knowing that a child he had with Tamar would not count as his own, spills his seed rather than impregnating Tamar. This failure to comply with the levirate law displeases God, so God strikes Onan dead as well. Because Tamar doesn't get pregnant and Judah's first two sons have died, in Judah's mind she must be cursed, so he refuses to give her to his third son. Judah sends Tamar back to her father's house. Judah plans a trip to look after his sheep, which Tamar hears about. She takes advantage of this window of opportunity and disguises herself. Judah runs into her and takes Tamar to be a prostitute. She sleeps with Judah and, for her services, will be paid a goat, but in the meantime she convinces Judah to leave some personal belongings as collateral (ring, cloak, and staff). When Judah sends his friend back to pay the prostitute, no one has ever heard of her. After some time Judah hears that Tamar has gotten pregnant, and has done so through harlotry. So Judah commands that she be brought forth to him for punishment. Tamar presents the ring, the cloak, and the staff and says these belong to the father of her child. Judah then realizes he is caught and declares that Tamar is more righteous than himself.

In a patriarchal society with few options for women, Tamar talks back and takes care of herself, not settling for the way things are. She makes her own way and carves out a future for herself in spite of the odds stacked against her. She does not whine about her circumstances or give up. She wheels and deals to wrest some kind of justice. The word used for Tamar's act is *sãd?qã*, an action that may not appear righteous in one context, but that may become a means of doing justice in another.[18] In a sermon on Tamar, Rev. Lindley DeGarmo points out that according to the text, Tamar is the great-grandmother of Jesus, and that this new, risky brand of righteousness is just what Jesus came to bring.[19]

Miriam is mostly known only through her brother Moses, but she was a leader in her own right. In Exodus 15:20 she is named a prophet. Her name shares the same root as the Greek name Mary, which means rebellion or hope of change.[20] Israel's deliverance from Egypt is attributed to her along with Moses and Aaron. According to the story in Numbers 12:1–15, in the face of competition, Miriam committed the unthinkable. She sassed God. She questioned Moses' leadership, challenging him for marrying a foreigner, a Cushite. Miriam and Aaron seek recognition of their own leadership: "Has the Lord spoken only through Moses?" That seems to have bought her a punishment of leprosy or some skin disease, according to the text. Yet it may not have been so much the fact that she talked back, but because she was unsupportive of Moses and untrusting of God.

Aaron who was guilty of the same thing was spared. Miriam alone bore the curse, standing in a long line of women who have been punished or humiliated for doing the same thing as their male counterparts.[21] Why was Aaron spared? Was it because men wrote the Bible? Was it because Miriam started the problem? Katharine Doob Sakenfeld suggests that it was because it would be unthinkable for Aaron, a male priest, to contract such a disease that renders one unclean.[22] Some biblical writers understood God as intolerant of anyone who questioned, particularly a woman, and tried to quell that. Yes, Miriam was jealous. Her failings are evident, but rather than condemning her insolence, we might praise her audacity. For in talking back to God, she was in fact claiming the covenant, defining her relationship with God and refusing to be ignored. She was cast out for seven days but then restored. We, like Miriam, cannot expect to exercise such chutzpa without consequences.

Again, the usual assumption has been that no one should ever question God. After all, look what happened to Job, right? This leads to the conclusion that God causes suffering as punishment. Modern biblical scholarship refutes this reading of Job's story. Darrell J. Fasching says the book of Job speaks more profoundly about chutzpah than any other book. Bruce Birch, Walter Brueggemann, et al., call it the principle of theodic protest.[23] Job evolves from a pious man to an angry, defiant one. According to Balentine: "He [Job] does not accept his misery passively; he questions God about its rightness. He does not confess his sin and return contritely to God; he attacks God with accusations that shake the very foundations of faith commitments."[24]

Job is forced to rethink his past assumptions. God is not an arbitrary authority who punishes Job just to prove might and power. God does not double that punishment because Job talks back. His sufferings are more of a description of the reality of the world. God, above all else, is beyond our understanding. Job's model of God at the beginning, as one who rewards goodness, is fair and equal, and has rightly blessed Job, is inadequate. God does not fit this prescribed role. Conventional explanations for his suffering do not suffice. Job's wife urges Job to curse God and acknowledge the failure of his trite explanations. Job's warnings to God call for a showdown. He does not crawl or beg, but demands an answer from God.[25] Yet God doesn't really give one. God speaks of creative power, not human concepts of justice. Job must come out in a new place, a transformation wrought from the chutzpah he had to find within himself.

In her book *Journey Through the Psalms,* Hebrew Bible scholar Denise Dombkowski Hopkins talks about what Roland Murphy has called "the art of complaining in faith," evident in the lament psalms.[26] The underappreciated laments are a rich source for the tradition of chutzpa. The lament tradition is described as "holding to God against God."[27] The language of lament recognizes harm and injustice, does not deny it, does not consent to it. It is a language of resistance and hope. Lament forces acknowledgment of hurt and pain. According to Marjorie Proctor-Smith, it is prayer of refusal to yield to and accept "the terror of things-as-they-are."[28] Hopkins recognizes the connection between the sass evident in black women's slave narratives and the chutzpah of the psalm laments. Sass involves "wit, courage, self-defense, speaking of truth, moral challenges—that defined themselves and dismantled the images that had been used to demean them." This language of sass is present in black literature, according to Hopkins, such as in Alice Walker's *The Color Purple* when Celie declares, "Let 'im hear me, I say. If [God] ever listened to poor colored women, the world would be a different place, I can tell you."[29] These "sass traditions," I maintain, are exactly the talk we need in ministry.

Faith communities and individuals in the Bible also relate to each other with chutzpa. Think of the gall of the prophets. Amos, a shepherd, received a call from God and traveled to Beth-el, the royal sanctuary of Israel, where he proceeded to condemn King Jereboam and his powerful leaders. Amos spoke out against a situation where a few knew prosperity at the expense of others:

> I hate, I despise your festivals, and I take no delight in your solemn assemblies. Even though you offer me your burnt offerings and grain offerings, I will not accept them; and the offerings of well-being of your fatted animals I will not look upon. Take away from me the noise of your songs; I will not listen to the melody of your harps. But let justice roll down like waters, and righteousness like an everflowing stream. (Amos 5: 21–24)

The prophets were notorious back talkers. The prophetic charsm makes them very difficult to live with, yet without prophecy, God's people would perish. They denounced injustice and wrongdoing and grieved over Israel. They longed for change and served to mobilize and encourage change. Tereza Cavalcanti notes the prophetic ministry of women in the Bible despite the system that favored men. Besides Miriam, there is Hulda (2 Kings 22:14). who prophesied against idolatry; Deborah (Judges 4:4), a judge who tells military leader Barak, what to do. (Wise man to come to her for advice!) She encouraged the people not to give up the struggle.[30] Marcia Y. Riggs documents the prophetic religious tradition of African American women in *Can I Get a Witness? Prophetic Religious Voices of African American Women: An Anthology.* This prophetic tradition operates to create what Walter Brueggerman has called "a destabilizing presence . . . so that alternatives are thinkable, so that the absolute claim of the system can be criticized."[31]

Prophets like Jeremiah condemn corruption and indulgence on the part of the people:

> Do not trust in these deceptive words: This is the temple of the Lord. . . . For if you truly amend your ways and your doings, if you execute justice one with another, if you do not oppress the alien, the [orphan] or the widow, or shed innocent blood in this place, and if you do not go after other gods to your own hurt, then I will dwell with you in this place. (Jeremiah 7:4f)

They also call God into question and speak judgements against God, demanding God's mercy. Habakkuh demands:

> How long, Lord shall I cry
> for help,
> and you will not listen?
> Or cry to you "Violence!"
> and you will not save?
> (Habakkuk 1:1–2)

To the prophets God was very real and very present. Their boldness in prayer reflected that intimacy.

The New Testament suggests a tradition of chutzpa as well. Stories told around Jesus' life and ministry reveal it. At least two parables indicate that chutzpa was part of the tradition about the teachings of Jesus. Luke 11:1–13 describes the tenacity of one who visits a friend at midnight and instructs us to ask, seek, knock. If you ask for a fish, God won't give you a snake. Luke 18 tells of a widow who keeps going back to a judge, demanding justice.[32] We are led to believe that we should be so persistent and relentless before God. Jesus often utilized the strategy of counterquery, answering a question with a question. His friend Martha dared to ask Jesus why he was distracting her sister from helping with the housework. She learned from Jesus that it is possible to be distracted by untempered service to others, and one must balance action and reflection. But if she had not questioned, she would not have learned. You have to admire the incorrigible Martha, who chastised Jesus again for coming late when her brother Lazarus was ill, blaming Jesus for his death. Yet almost in the same breath she professes her faith in Christ. Perhaps only one with such profound doubt is capable of such profound faith.

Although Jesus' whole life in some ways modeled back talk, one primary example is the story of him turning over the tables of the money changers in the temple. This passage is not to be regarded as denouncing Jewish practices as it often has been. Jesus was protesting complacent religion and hypocrisy. His action was not merely a protest against the presence of money in God's house, but of the misplaced priorities of some who were superficially religious. God's presence had been signified in the temple, and he "turns over" this situation and takes the place of the temple. Before the marginalized had been cast out, Jesus welcomed the stranger, the blind, the lame. In the gospel accounts of this story, especially John, there seems to be a good bit of righteous anger attributed to Jesus, a contrast to the prevalent meek and mild image. The story attests to the need for agents of change and for honest dissension from accepted, unmindful practice.

Jesus talked back to religious leaders:

> Woe to you scribes and Pharisees, hypocrites! For you tithe mint and cummin, and have neglected the weightier matters of the law, justice and mercy and faith: these you ought to have done without neglecting the others. (Matthew 23:23)

We also know of the pleading laments of Jesus at the end of his life, in the Garden of Gethsemane and from the cross. While he took on his suffering and the role he was to have in human salvation, he did not do it without questioning in Matthew 27:46, "My God, my God, why have you forsaken me?"

I conclude two things about back talk in the Bible. First, although I have shown numerous examples of chutzpa (but not all of them), there are, of course, many other examples of a lack of guts, especially the wimpiness of God's people. That is, in fact, the prevailing view in Christian spiritually, that we are powerless before God, that we can only submit and be silent— that we should just sit back and take what is coming to us. It seems the tradition of chutzpa was soon lost. My point is not to deny our need to yield before our creator, but to balance that with the recognition and recovery of back-talking traditions. When we stand before God, we recognize that we have less power than God, but we are not powerless.

Secondly, back talk is a dangerous, risky business. We may feel punished and persecuted. We will suffer. We may end up with a limp. No one should ever talk back without expecting consequences. That should never stop us. It did not stop Tamar, Miriam, Job, Jesus, some early mothers and fathers of the church, the reformers, or even Susan B. Anthony, Sojourner Truth, Ghandi, Dietrich Bonhoeffer, Martin Luther King, Jr., Nelson Mandala, or myriads of others who refused to accept the "terror-of-things-as-they-are."

Suppression in the Early Church

The squelching of defiant talk, the insistence that everyone speak univocally was deemed necessary for the good of the Christian church. Dissonant voices, especially those of women, and counterspeech was quickly condemned as heresy. Etymologically, in ancient Greek, the verb "hairein," meaning "to take," gave rise to the adjective hairetos, which meant "able to choose," and the noun "hairesis," which meant "the act of choosing" from which the word heresy comes. In time the noun developed the extended senses of a choice, a course of action, a school of thought, and a philosophical or religious sect. Stoicism, for example, was a hairesis. Within Judaism, a "heresy" (our modern English equivalent) was a religious faction, part, or sect, such as the Pharisees or Sadducees. Applied to such groups, hairesis was used in a neutral, nonpejorative manner.[33] Eventually the ability to choose, to make decisions for oneself evolved into heresy, understood pejoratively. The effort to reconstruct a more just picture of women's leadership in the history of the church has to overcome the traditional understandings of what is normative and what is heretical.[34]

Another suppression was the subjugation of women and their leadership, which was reinforced by the identification of God with patriarchal values, dominance, and hierarchy.[35] Recent research, however, has unearthed how women served as formal and informal leaders in the early church and how they talked back to a tradition that tried to silence them. Though chutzpa was discouraged, we can acknowledge and appreciate women's leadership in the church from the earliest times.

Though I cannot attempt to give a comprehensive history of women in ministry here, some broad brush strokes provide insight into the developing understanding of the contributions of women. Deborah F. Sawyer notes the difficulty in reconstructing this history because of the lack of direct evidence from women themselves, since men were the ones who wrote ancient history. She examines unconventional sources, archeological evidence, and practices reading texts "against the grain," without reading in contemporary agendas on women and religion.[36] Sawyer contrasts Greek and Roman attitudes toward women. By Greek custom women were more submissive and lived in almost total seclusion, whereas Roman women were more high profile and engaged in public life.[37] Though Judaism was a cultic system that was allowed to exist during the Roman empire, its attitudes toward women reflected its ancient laws and practices.

Writing in the first century C.E., Philo, the Jewish philosopher, described women in Judaism as "best suited to the indoor life" and responsible for practices that made for a Jewish home. Male children were distinctly preferred over female babies. Laws from the Torah dictated that women's menstrual flow made her unclean for seven days during which time women were isolated from men. Feminists have argued that this taboo and isolation was a means of patriarchal control over women.[38] According to tradition, women were restricted to the Court of Women in the Temple, but men were allowed to pass through this court. Even so, women were involved in cultic practices that were inherited from ancient civilizations, according to Sawyer. One piece of evidence is an inscription from Tell el-Yahudiyyeh in Egypt, the site of a temple, that named a woman "priestess." Sawyer conjectures that the Greco-Roman environment, particularly Egypt, the home of the Isis cult, did influence Judaism by allowing women of priestly families to function as priests. Sawyer also raised the question about whether women really were as separated and restricted in religious practice as thought.[39]

Most Christians today, according to Karen Jo Torjesen, including clergy and scholars, presume that women had very little role in the spread of Christianity. But women did, in fact, have a crucial role in Jesus' ministry and were prominent leaders in the early church. She contends that the Christian church did not suddenly spring up with a well-developed organizational structure but started out as a social movement.[40] Jesus both depended upon Jewish sources and challenged accepted practices of the time. His vision of a new "community of equals" replaced the patriarchal and hierarchical structure. In this charismatic, new community, the Spirit of God took precedence over hierarchy. Gospel sayings reveal that Jesus valued women. Sawyer contends that the eschatological perspectives of the Jesus movement that hoped for the new radical domain of justice may account for such inclusive attitudes toward women.[41]

Feminist historians in the '80s and '90s have sought to unearth women's presence and role in Jesus' ministry and afterwards. Evidence of women priests may be found in an epistle of Pope Gelasius in the late fifth century. This pope condemns the bishops who conferred priestly ordination on women. The four church councils (Nicaea, Laodicea, Mimes, and Orange) in the fourth and fifth centuries took great measure to ban the ordination of women, implying that this was indeed the practice. Historians are rediscovering art that depicts women among Jesus' followers and in prominent roles of preaching, teaching, and leading worship.

A fresco from an early Roman catacomb appears to depict women celebrating the Lord's Supper. The bodies, hair, and dress indicate they are women. The figure actually breaking the bread wears distinctively female dress, though the face appears to have been sanded down.[42] A third-century fresco shows a woman probably leading public prayer.[43] Joan Morris describes the Church of St. Praxedis in Rome that may date back to apostolic times. There is a mosaic with the word "Episcopa" over the head of a woman. The name "Theodora" in stonework has obviously been changed to the male form "Theodo." The title "Theodora Episcopa" appears on a column outside the chapel.[44] In contrast to the depiction of Mary Magdalene as a harlot in much of Renaissance art, a twelfth-century painting shows her preaching to the Apostles, and a fifteenth-century bas relief located in the Cathedral of Vieille Major in Marseilles shows her preaching to the princes of Marseilles. Also, new art and artists show women and children as equal partners, such as that produced by Avoca Publishing in Ireland.

During the birthing of the church, as the apostles and others began to proselytize, women participated actively in leadership roles by providing homes where the house churches could meet, and as congregational leaders, prophets, and evangelists. Some evidence for the involvement of women in the Pauline communities comes from the Pauline texts. In his letter to the Christians in Rome, Paul mentions Phoebe, a deacon who helped his ministry. Phoebe was identified as his *prostatis,* a title that means leader or president, according to Elisabeth Schüssler Fiorenza.[45] He greets Prisca and names Junia as a fellow apostle (Romans 16:7). Acts makes mention of Lydia, a wealthy businesswoman who offered her home to the apostles. In Philippians 4:2 Paul names Euodia and Syntyche as working side-by-side with him.

Karen L. King lists women who served as leaders in house churches, holding offices and acting as prophets. She writes: "As prophets, women's roles would have included not only ecstatic public speech, but preaching, teaching, leading prayer and perhaps even performing the eucharist meal."[46]

Other writings such as apocryphal books and Egyptian texts name women who served as leaders in a variety of ways. Judith is one who acted in a manner "normally reserved in biblical narrative for men." [47] Another is Thecla, a virgin who ran away from home and took up preaching. Women such as Perpetua were also martyred along with men. King notes that there were, of course, many others whose names are lost to us. Martyrdom in a way abolished sex roles and gave women a "manly spirit" to fight and die alongside their brothers.[48] The African church father Tertullian, for example, famous for his hostility to women leaders, apparently accepted women prophets. He described an unnamed woman who had ecstatic visions during church services and noted her service as a counselor and healer.[49]

New Testament Epistles indicate, however, that women leaders were accepted in some locations but not in others. They were more generally recognized in the Eastern church than in the Western church. Roger Gryson writes: "Since women were not permitted 'to teach or have authority over men,' they were naturally excluded in Pastoral Epistles from the functions of *episkopos* and presbyter, whose purpose was the management and instruction of the community."[50]

A tension developed in these charismatic communities in the need for more structure to help with communication and the spread of the gospel. A community based on charisma was subject to abuse and could and did lead to spiritual conceit. Measures were taken to try to prevent that from happening. Strong opposition to the leadership of women is found in several New Testament passages (Colossians 3:18; Ephesians 5:21–33; Titus 2:3–5; I Timothy 2:8–15; 5:3–16; I Corinthians 14: 33b–36). These passages, according to Barbara J. MacHaffie, "do not describe the status of women in all churches, but instead try to impose upon the Christian communities the patriarchal standards of the ancient world."[51] As the church grew, the influence of the culture began to shape the structure and governance of the church. Women's status in these communities declined with the rise of hierarchical structures. The tradition of women leaders who dedicated their lives to the gospel certainly continued, but their leadership became more and more marginalized. Deborah Sawyer contends that these attitudes toward women that developed when Christianity began to define itself over against Judaism became definitive and remain so for much of the Western world today.[52]

Regardless, some women co-workers of Paul and the widows "strike a chord of dissonance within their society" by wishing to exercise some of the freedoms that men enjoyed to preach the gospel, which they believed fervently. They were convinced that they had been so transformed by the death and resurrection of Jesus as to make their teaching, preaching, and leadership as effective as that of men.[53]

Out of Paul's charge to the churches to care for widows, there eventually developed orders of women who were supported by the community and in turn performed some particular leadership functions such as instruction for baptism and care for the sick. This eventually gave rise to feminine monasticism, which preceded its male counterpart.[54] Although the widows and virgins were honored for their holy orders, they still were denied public leadership positions. Perhaps the group that comes closest to official leadership is the deaconesses. Manuscript and archaeological evidence coming especially from the Eastern churches in places like Jerusalem, Syria, Greece, and Asia Minor present a clear record of this ministry.[55] At least on the surface a deaconess was considered to be on the same level as a male deacon, and both were ordained to serve as teachers, supervisors, to visit the sick, and to perform a variety of other functions. The deaconesses, however, had restrictions on what they could do and where and to whom they could minister. They could assist at the baptism of a woman but not a man because, at that time, a baptismal candidate's entire body was anointed. Thus the deaconesses were charged with teaching and anointing the female candidates. They were not allowed to pronounce the words of baptism in the ritual itself.[56]

Church Women Through the Ages

In subsequent centuries most historical accounts see the public role of women and their influence continuing to decline. Formal education was reserved for men, and the economic gap widened between the rich and the poor. Wealthy women exercised some leadership through patronage, or helping men of a lower social standing. In this way women gained political power by winning the loyalty of those they helped financially. A few women of the ruling classes were able to have political sway but generally through their husbands. As Karen Jo Torjesen notes, a woman's virtues were chastity, silence, and obedience.[57]

Images of women that emerged in medieval documents present two conflicting views of women, according to Barbara MacHaffie. In many cases women are denounced as foolish, inferior, or even as witches. In others women are praised and idealized. Misogynism led to or was fueled in part by a fear of women and their sexuality. Women were associated with evil and the devil because of their sexual lure to men and their reproductive powers. Many women chose the lifestyle of asceticism, which promoted chastity and monasticism. This way of life afforded women some freedom denied to them in church and society, such as traveling and making pilgrimages. Women were also involved in the spiritual movement of medieval Christian mysticism such as Julian of Norwich, Mechthild of Magdebury, Catherine of Siena, and Hildegard of Bingen. Mysticism may have recognized women's religious experience as beyond the control of men. These women were known to have advised the hierarchy on spiritual matters.[58] The monasteries for women were headed by women (abbesses) like Hilda of Whitby or Etheldreda of Ely. This provided them an opportunity for leadership within the institutional confines of the church. The word "ordination" was sometimes used to describe the consecration of an abbess. Though not given the authority to administer the sacraments, these women were given the same symbols of high office as a bishop, such as a ring, mitre, and crozier. The power of the abbesses declined, however, in the late Middle Ages.[59]

Early reformers believed that the Bible commanded the subordination of women and so continued the rejection of women's leadership. Reformers did lessen the association of women and sexuality with evil. Though Luther asserted a belief in "the priesthood of all believers," he did not find that women had the gifts to preach. In spite of this, some women actively participated in the reform movement.[60]

The rise of the Puritan sects brought little freedom to women. The subjugation of women was carried on in the colonies as well. The fear of witchcraft from the Middle Ages lingered on. Learning for women continued to be discouraged. Women were expected to attend worship (often worshiping separately from men). Women could not be ministers in the Anglican and Puritan traditions. A few well-known women such as Anne Hutchinson began to read and expound on theology. Anne was unjustly excommunicated as an Antinomian, one who opposed salvation by good works and adherence to moral laws. The Quakers encouraged women to engage in ministry and missionary activity. From their beginnings Quakers acknowledged the equality of men and women in every aspect of life including ministry. Margaret Fell was one such important female Quaker leader and preacher. The Quakers have a doctrine of the Inner Light, which can come to women as well as men.[61]

Gradually more girls and women learned to read. In the revivalist tradition with its evangelical style, marked in America by the First Great Awakening in the 1740s, women found greater opportunity for participation and leadership in the Christian community. Evangelicals stressed the experience of conversion, and women as well as men could publicly share their witness about their religious experience, though some men cautioned women against such open leadership.[62] In Methodism women engaged in public speaking and were active as class leaders and teachers. Over the course of his life, John Wesley began to recognize the contributions of women and their ability to win souls, so he eventually encouraged some of them to preach. Sarah Mallet, Hester Ann Roe, Mary Bosanquet, Sarah Crosby, and Elizabeth Ritchie traveled around to preach, and Wesley supported them. During the nineteenth century, the Holiness Movement was one of the instrumental forces behind women feeling called to preach. Phoebe Palmer was a prolific advocate for women's right to preach, and she wrote and spoke extensively, using biblical passages in her arguments. Frances Willard, famous educator and temperance crusader, also defended the woman's right to be in the pulpit. The Holiness Movement helped prepare the way for women's ordination.[63] Late-nineteenth and-twentieth century African American women such as Maria Steward, Nannie Helen Burroughs, and Olivia B. Stokes contributed significant leadership to the black church.

Women and Ordination

Congregational and Unitarian churches were the first to accept women's ordination in the 1850s, but only a few served as pastors until much later. There was also an increase in women engaged in formalized work in the church in missions, education, or social work. Theological education for women was a problem because most seminaries were closed to them. Training schools opened to prepare women for mission education and social work. Seminaries gradually opened to women in the twentieth century, at first mostly so they could prepare to become professional educators in the church. Women experienced and recognized their call to serve as teachers and also as pastors.

Antoinette Brown is generally thought to be the first woman formally ordained to the Christian ministry. She fulfilled the requirements for a theological degree from Oberlin College but was not allowed to receive the degree. (Many years later she was given an honorary degree.) She was called to a small Congregationalist Church in New York in 1853 where she was ordained.[64] In 1878, Anna Howard Shaw became the second woman to graduate from Boston University School of Theology, but she was refused ordination by the Methodist Episcopal Church. She persisted, turning to the Methodist Protestant Church where, after much debate, she was ordained in October 1880. She served two small churches in Massachusetts for seven years until she left to begin work with the women's suffrage movement.[65]

Following Anna Howard Shaw were many women who served as licensed preachers, but ordination was slow, and full ordination rights were not granted by the Methodists until 1956. Some Presbyterian bodies were also ordaining women by the 1950s and 1960s. The Lutheran Church in America (and the American Lutheran Church) voted to ordain women in 1970.

In the 1960s and 1970s, with the launch of the feminist movement, more women came to realize they had options, and they increasingly paid attention to and responded to the call to ministry. With the influx of women into the seminaries and into the pastorate, and as more women began to serve as liturgical leaders, there came a call for inclusive worship language. Although some argued that "mankind" for people and "He" for God actually included women and was simply a grammatical convenience, feminists maintained that it really did not include them at all. The mid-1970s brought efforts to find ways to read the Bible and worship more inclusively, reclaiming feminine imagery and words for the Divine.

The first woman to be ordained in the Anglican communion, according to Pamela W. Darling, was Florence Li Tim-Oi, who was priested in 1944 by Ronald O. Hall, the bishop of Hong Kong. She was ordained specifically to minister to Chinese Anglicans under the Japanese Occupation. Her ordination, however, was denounced by the Church of England, and she agreed to "suspend her sacramental ministry" so punitive action would not be taken against Bishop Hall.[66] The Episcopal Church in the U.S. officially sanctioned women's ordination in 1976 in a vote of the House of Deputies in Minneapolis.[67] The Church of England voted to ordain women on November 11, 1992. Again, unofficially, women of the Anglican communion in many countries preached, led worship, witnessed to their faith, taught, and ministered to the sick and bereaved.

Prior to the vote in the Church of England, some leaders formed the Movement for the Ordination of Women (MOW), which had both male and female members. This para-church organization became critical to the change in attitudes and policy. Though not much information is available to us about the strategies that denominations used to obtain ordination rights for women, one assumes that similar organizations existed and played a role. MOW evolved into WATCH (Women and the Church), which now advocates for women in ministry and for opening the episcopacy to women in the Church of England, where there is still a ban on women bishops. Two years after the 1992 vote, 1,280 women were priested by the Church of England. Those present recalled some protests outside, but they were more struck by the Roman Catholic women (and perhaps men) cheering on their sisters.[68]

Rosemary Radford Ruether has traced the role of women in Roman Catholic Christianity. While feminism "moved into the churches" in the 1970s, the magisterium persisted in rejecting women's ordination, and the Roman Catholic Church remains one of the few hold outs in Christendom. In 1976 the Vatican issued its "Declaration on the Question of the Admission of Women to the Ministerial Priesthood," perhaps in response to the American Episcopal Church's vote to ordain women. This document argues that the refusal to ordain women is not because the church is discriminating against women, but because the nature of women is incompatible with the priesthood. It further argues that Jesus purposely did not include women in ordained ministry, and that the priest represents Christ, who was male.[69] Women are not ordainable because maleness is necessary to the sacramental representation of Christ, according to the document. Christ represents God: God is male. One wonders exactly what it is about maleness that is necessary to represent God?

Soon after the declaration came out, several scholars condemned it. Karl Rahner denounced such literalism about the maleness of Christ. Rahner stated that despite papal approval and the claim that the ban is "unchangeable," it is not a definitive decision and is in principle reformable.[70] David Willis contends that there are such compelling biblical and theological reasons for ordaining women that the burden of proof is now on those who do not. He says that the ordination of women is an "effective sign of the new Creation in Christ."[71] Formal policy regarding women's ordination is one thing whereas actual practice is another. Despite the ban on women's ordination in the Roman Catholic Church, its clergy shortage has meant that many parishes in the U.S. have been led by women in pastoral roles. The Vatican has issued a statement disapproving such lay leadership that many feel was aimed at women.[72]

The St. Joan's International Alliance, a Roman Catholic feminist organization founded in 1910 in England, fought for women's suffrage and raised the issue of the role of women in Roman Catholic leadership.[73] The U.S. Catholic Women's Ordination movement and the Women's Ordination Conference (WOC) founded in 1974 continues to mobilize for the cause. Their Project Priesthood identifies women who believe themselves called to the priesthood and are responsible for the great bumper stickers that say "Ordain us or quit baptizing us," and "Ordain us or quit dressing like us." The WOC has confronted bishops and even the pope.

Ruether asserts that polls indicate that more than 60 percent of U.S. Catholics support women's ordination. It is an uphill battle, however. Roman Catholic priests who dissent on this issue are not advanced to the episcopacy, and theologians that teach in many Catholic colleges and universities are required to receive a mandatum from a bishop that may include acceptance of the ban on women's ordination. John Wijngaards, perhaps the only Roman Catholic priest to resign in protest to the church's ban on the ordination of women, has authored a book, *The Ordination of Women in the Catholic Tradition: Unmasking a Cuckoo's Egg Tradition,* which examines and critiques Rome's arguments. Another Catholic priest, however, told me that the Church has come to see the light on other issues. When liberation theologies first began to proliferate, the magisterium flatly condemned those writings, he said, but later produced a document that began "As the Church has always professed . . . " and then picked up the exact liberation language it had once condemned.

Rosemary Ruether reports that radical wings of Catholic feminism now question whether ordination is a desirable goal since it is ordination into a patriarchal church. It is precisely when feminists discover the truly liberating message of the Gospel that they seem to experience their greatest alienation from existing churches. They have organized "womenchurch" communities.[74] I personally am struck by groups of women who gather to worship on their own terms, who do not need male supervision.

Ada María Isasi-Díaz tells of LAS HERMANAS, a twenty-year-old international Hispanic woman's organization. This group has struggled with the issue of celebrating mass at its meetings because of the exclusion of women from ordained ministry in the Catholic Church. They have developed their own liturgies and rituals around Jesus as compañero in the struggle.[75] Rebecca Chopp, however, cautions that separatism does not transform the structures of patriarchy and may function to maintain the status quo. Yet she recognizes the visionary force of the new ecclesia that is not for women only.[76] Because the church in Korea still has a male-centered ministry, women are gathering, often in secret, keeping active in their original churches as well as in the new womenchurch communities. Ruether sees womenchurch as leading the exodus from patriarchy. The feminist liturgies of these communities are indeed a brilliant form of back talk.[77] Some women talk back through their "staying power" (to borrow Carter Heyward's phrase); others talk back by leaving. Both forms of witness are needed. The ordination of women, need not be seen as their tacit approval of patriarchal structures that excluded women for so many years, but rather as a challenge to any such exclusion.

I have to say that among some ordained Protestant women I have seen a lack of empathy and solidarity for our Roman Catholic sisters. There is a "we fought our battle, now you have to fight your own" sentiment, or there is the tacit assumption that women who want to be ordained should leave the Roman Catholic Church. I think that is misguided and does nothing to change the church, to call it to be an "effective sign of the new creation." As one Catholic woman put it, "I am still a Catholic, and I refuse to be driven away from the community I claim as home."[78]

The issue of women's ordination in the Roman Catholic Church, therefore, is not off the table. Rosemary Ruether writes:

> Although the Vatican may try to hold the line on acceptance of these modern views, it is unlikely that they will convince the majority of Catholics. It may be only a matter of time before church teaching adapts itself to modern times and also to the deeper liberation vision of Christianity, but this remains to be seen.[79]

In this chapter I have called upon the expressive biblical tradition of chutzpa for its wisdom and insight into the persistence of women's leadership in the Christian faith. I have briefly traced the trajectory of that persistence through church history, despite the omission or misappropriation of women's leadership by patriarchal interpreters. One could rightly suppose that there is much more to tell. Back talkers are not and never have been just a few talking heads.

▪ 4 ▪

TALKING US THROUGH IT
Stories and Strategies for Change

THE FOLLOWING NARRATIVES tell how some leaders brought about change in the church and survived! These ethnographic studies are mostly about women, told from their perspective, but they involve men leaders as well. According to Rebecca Chopp, women must develop new discourses for their lives, writing and speaking their stories, not through the "closure of an eternal division between men and women, but through adventure, laughter, openness, freedom, creativity and friendship."[1]

These stories reveal that these women have the right stuff of leadership, that they learn from living, and they sincerely desire to fulfill God's call on their lives. The stories are different, but they have some commonalties. The stories lead to strategies that reveal what worked and how.

The women talked about bucking the system with grace. Some did not think of themselves as exercising a particular method for change or using back talk. They did not see themselves as research specimens, but in looking back on what they accomplished, they agreed that back talk was part of what they did.

These leaders were very humble about what they accomplished and were reluctant to brag about it. They were just doing what they had to do. There are no foolproof methods. No one strategy is perfect. Leadership is not walking a fine line of appropriate techniques. You will notice that the strategies often have a paradoxical quality to them, and effective leaders understand that paradox. Marjorie Procter-Smith makes an insightful comparison between feminist strategies and cooking. Cooking is not just repeating technique created by others, unimaginative and pedestrian. Cooking is more like alchemy, the blending of elements into something wonderful.[2] Too much or too little of something makes a difference. Like cooking, leadership requires goals of transformation. Yet the strategies call us beyond standing still. In some ways the strategies are common sense, but in other ways they challenge us to see things from a new perspective and to think and act creatively.

How Change Occurred in the Northern Virginia Baptist Association

Rev. Dr. Janice Jenkins told me the story of how the 124-year-old Northern Virginia Baptist Association (NVBA) recently came to ordain women preachers and to include them as full members in their ranks. Although another Baptist woman said that one does not usually mention change and the Baptist church in the same breath, this subtitle is not an oxymoron.

Janice related the long debate within the Baptist denomination concerning the role of women. She said that most of the time in the discussions there had been "more heat than light."[3] The NVBA is a black church association, a union consisting of many African American Baptist churches in Northern Virginia. The association is governed by a hierarchy of elected, ordained male preachers. The moderator is its CEO, and an annual session is held to determine the association's policies and agenda.

The NVBA enjoys a rich history of spreading the gospel and doing God's work. Historically, only men were allowed to be members. While the body's constitution did not explicitly forbid women's membership and ordination, the unwritten policy was understood—a hard, fast, and unquestioned rule, according to Janice.[4] Women attended sessions with their husbands but were seen and not heard. Janice reported that churches with women pastors have been denied membership in the NVBA. Even though in Baptist polity the authority to ordain rests with individual congregations, some churches were forced to rescind their membership because they ordained women.

In 1938 an auxiliary group, The Baptist Women's Convention of Northern Virginia, was organized with the permission and blessing of the association. The terminology is intentional; women had to get permission to organize. The women's convention took a deep interest in home and foreign missions and exerted influence (if a quiet one) on the association. In 1952 the Women's Convention helped to purchase land for both a new center to be constructed to house the offices of the association as well as a camping and retreat facility. Dr. Jenkins indicates that the Women's Convention exerted power through its financial support of the Baptist Center. The NVBA's stand toward women's ordination and membership, however, was not really publicly questioned until 1997.

In 1997, Rev. Kenny Smith became the fifteenth moderator of the NVBA. He had not sought the office but was elected after circumstances prevented other candidates from accepting it. When his name was put forth, he was elected enthusiastically. Moderator Smith had some new ideas for the association, and people were excited about his leadership. Janice Jenkins came to take a more active leadership role in the NVBA, as she felt the call from God. She worked with Kenny Smith, who was also the pastor of her church, and he encouraged her leadership.

Moderator Smith expressed to the NVBA the need to deal with some underlying tension concerning women in ministry. Women were increasingly becoming active in the association but were still informally barred as full participants. Rev. Jenkins thinks that the blockade against women was theological. Many well-meaning Baptists, including women, have been taught and believe that God excludes women from ministry and from the pulpit, taking the words from Ephesians to apply to the church today. A minority of people in the NVBA did not hold this view. Moderator Smith was among that minority. He put forth a four-year theme for the working of the association entitled: "Unity: Many Members, One Body." Preaching and teaching were variations on this theme. His hope was to raise the issue of women's ministry in the NVBA.

Moderator Smith, when recalling the process of change in the association, said he did not want to split the NVBA or alienate members. In his mind he had the four-year plan to move the association to a new place in regards to women in ministry. The presence of women increased. In his third year in office, Moderator Smith brought a woman pastor to preach at the annual session. It was a first for them. It is interesting, according to Jenkins, that because it seemed such a natural thing to do, many people did not even realize that it was the first time a woman had preached at the NVBA's annual session.

A symposium was held in October 2000 on the question of whether women belonged in the pastoral ministry. There was a panel discussion and several days of speakers and debates. Moderator Smith urged all to "disagree agreeably." At the symposium the NVBA called for a vote at the next annual session on whether women could be full participants in the association and whether they could be ordained. Several leaders stood up and objected to a vote being taken. One church leader argued that "if we ordain women, we will see a decline in membership." Another responded, "I don't think we will, but so what if we do? Are we faithful to the Gospel?"

The body did eventually call for a vote. At the 124th Annual Session of the NVBA in May 2001, history was made at the Baptist Center. Following several speakers, worship services, and an address from the moderator, the NVBA voted to include women in full membership and to allow the possibility of ordination. One hundred and eleven voted for women's membership and ordination. Fifty-seven voted against it. A few members resigned but not many. Since the association's constitution says nothing for or against the ordination of women, the vote was viewed by some as an amendment. Since Baptist churches are autonomous, the decision of the NVBA is not considered binding on member congregations. Yet many do follow the policies and decisions made by the collective body. For example, as Janice Jenkins told me, there was historical precedent from the civil rights movement. While the NVBA voted to support civil rights, it did not dictate to individual churches how to be involved. Jenkins believes that, like they did regarding civil rights, most member churches will follow the lead, the will, and the wisdom of the NVBA in regard to women's ordination.

In analyzing how the change occurred and what we can learn from it, I note first that a respected leader spoke out for change. Be it male or female, when change is needed, the gender of the back talker, while not irrelevant, takes a back seat to the task at hand. Women, of course, had a role in creating the change. Rev. Jenkins and several other women were the unofficial leaders of the movement for change. They networked with others inside and outside of the association to garner support. As an African American male, Rev. Smith's leadership for women in ministry was not motivated by self-interest, but by an interest in furthering the ministry of the church.

Recognizing the potential of the women in the NVBA, he told of the excitement and enthusiasm expressed at the Baptist General Conventions and other national bodies, where women have full participation and ordination. That excitement and enthusiasm was lacking in the NVBA. "We seemed to be spinning our wheels and doing the same old things, thinking the same old way," he said. Rev. Smith also credits education for his position on women in ministry, being persuaded while in seminary at Howard

University School of Divinity that who is called into the ministry is God's business.

In a course taught by Dr. Delores Carpenter, he wrestled with scripture that seemed to exclude women from leadership in the church, but that went against his own gut-level belief. He came to understand that part of the agenda for the pastoral epistles was to reinforce institutional consolidation in the early church and to develop the notions of authority and organization for the church. The submission of women was seen as necessary for institutional development reinforcing the accepted notions of women of that time, which are certainly not justified today, whether they were then or not. Other references to women as leaders and deacons suggested to him that women did have leadership and authority in the expansion of the church.

During his tenure, Moderator Smith provided many opportunities for people to learn and dialogue about this issue. First, he brought in speakers, teachers, and preachers on both sides of the issue. He was said to gradually wear down some of the resistance, and the controversy seemed, "well, less controversial." One member described his work as "smoothing away the sharp edges." Some might say that his actions were slow, but four years is a small price to pay for 124 years of rejection. It took four years for all voices to be heard. A steamroller approach could have set the cause of women in ministry back even further.

Secondly, a woman came forth and proclaimed her call to ministry. She was Linda Bullock of the First Baptist Church of Vienna, Virginia, a congregation that is a member of the NVBA. In the Baptist tradition, as in others, a person's role in the church is determined by the way the Holy Spirit is manifested in that person's life. One becomes a pastor not simply by choosing to, but only upon recognition from others that the Spirit has given this person the gifts and has empowered him or her for the pastoral ministry. The first requirement for pastoral ministry is manifestation of the spirit. Members of First Baptist in Vienna clearly recognized this in Linda Bullock and licensed her to preach. This event turned a key. "It was a big old door swung on its hinges," according to Janice Jenkins. "I could almost hear its creaking." More women began to express their call to ministry. While the frequency of an event does not necessarily validate it, it does cause one to question and re-evaluate long-held positions. Other women came forth in the NVBA and declared their call; some sought ordination.[5]

Rev. Jenkins has started a new church, the Judah Praise Fellowship Baptist Church. She was approved by the executive board of the NVBA to become a full member, the first female pastor to do so. She and Rev. Bessie T. Jett have been appointed to the NVBA's Ordination Council, again the first two women on this council.

Another factor in the change was the increased dissatisfaction with the treatment of women, in particular their exclusion from the Minister's Conference, a union of clergy within the NVBA. More and more grumbling could be heard about the lockout, according to Rev. Smith. Some African American males who themselves had been locked out and discriminated against could resonate with the women. The hypocrisy of the exclusionary treatment of women became more apparent. Janice concluded that "things just came together that made it possible for us to move forward."

This story has a happy ending, but the struggle for the ordination of women in Northern Virginia is not an isolated struggle—not "somebody's else's fight," but a victory for all. It is instructive to note how change can and does come when the time is right and how we can help that along. It gives us hope for further gains for women's leadership in the church and suggests some strategies that we can employ.

Strategy #1: Take Advantage of Tension and "The Right Time"

Moderator Smith talked about tension in the NVBA when he took office on the issue of women in ministry. He and the women leaders in the movement did not polarize the association but gave people on both sides a voice. A possible reason for the delay in accepting women leaders was suggested by Delores C. Carpenter. She points out how leadership in the black church for years was reserved for men because often there were few other opportunities for black men. When black women pushed for some say in the decision making, many of the men saw this as diminishing their power and control. Further, she says that the patriarchy is reinforced by women's desire for a strong spiritual leader, a desire to be around a "man of God."[6] But the call of women to ministry could not be squelched.

Tension and controversy can be painful, but they can also bring opportunity. Maria Harris wrote that tension might be understood not in the sense of something that causes stress and strain, but in the sense of tightness or tautness, a "positive condition created when important forces pull against each other." She writes, "The lack of tension causes collapse. Tension is needed. Tension is good."[7] She suggests that tensions in the church are many, and it is through tension that the community engages in reasoned and compassionate decision making. Tension signals that some movement is about to occur. Too much tension, however, and communication breaks down. One perspective becomes dominant and domineering.

Implementing times of tension is related to one of the eight steps to change and transformation named by leadership guru John P. Kotter. He says that leadership for change "establishes a sense of urgency." In times of natural tension, a good leader will confront reality and raise the bar as if to say, "This is the way it is, but this is the way it could be."[8] Rev. Smith did not rush through the process of examining the issues, as those of us impatient for change may be tempted to do. We want resolution. We want to win! He did, however, point out the tension and in so doing created a sense of urgency that something must change. Working in and through tension is part of the art of leadership. He recognized that women could bring something that the NVBA needed, and women stepped up to the plate.

Echoing this, one of the things that Rev. Patricia Farris, pastor of First United Methodist Church in Santa Monica, California, does to bring about change is to promote a sense of urgency. When she came to her parish four years ago it was in a slow, steady decline. The church, however, was large enough and so financially stable that nobody noticed. If they did, they just assumed the situation would rectify itself. She writes:

> None of us trying to help lead change can ever underestimate the magnitude of forces that reinforce complacency and help maintain the status quo. Inertia is a powerful force. . . . Change is not a neat and tidy process. It is not a linear process. . . . You cannot take a church to places it really doesn't want to go.[9]

Leaders can help the church to glimpse a new landscape and see the benefits of going there.

A sense of urgency is not a sense of anxiety and fear, to which if we are not careful, we can succumb. Rev. Farris got new leaders involved and talked with them about their observations of the needs in the church and community. Not buried too far under the surface was a potential groundswell. Back talk enters into this strategy as a means of creating that urgency. One can talk about and ask for change for a long time before anything happens. In the case of the NVBA, the talk that was behind the scenes for years emerged as open conversation. Like bell hooks explains, back talk became a rite of initiation, testing the courage of those who were engaging in it and moving them from being excluded to being inside the ranks of full membership. Back talk is the nucleus of the struggle. She writes: "We are rooted in language, wedded, have our being in words. Language is also a place of struggle. The oppressed struggle in language to recover ourselves—to rewrite, to reconcile, to renew. Our words are not without meaning. They are an action—a resistance."[10] Because language is so much a part of our identity, Janice Jenkins, Kenny Smith, and others sought change through endless conversation and made their language inclusive to model the inclusion of women in the NVBA.

If there is ever an expedient time for change in the church, it is now. We are on the verge of not being believed. Old ways and words are clearly not working to communicate the gospel in what Stephen Carter calls "a culture of disbelief."[11] The charismatic preacher whose message is "believe because I do and say you should" is no longer producing enduring results. Jesus did not attempt to persuade by eloquent speech or solely on the strength of his character. He called people into faith in God, into a life worth living, a life that defies the cultural norms of the day, a life that manifests grace. We are called to manifest grace in this time and place.

Strategy #2: Work With the Leadership

Rev. Smith was a successful member of the hierarchy and a male. What would he stand to gain from fighting for the ordination of women? He would stand to make a lot of enemies. It would have been simpler to go with the status quo, yet he did encourage change. Even though oppressed people cannot rely upon or wait for the oppressor to change, one cannot rule out any sincere ally. Women in the association saw Rev. Smith as a friend in the struggle, as one whom they could approach for change. It was strategic to have a male in their corner. But more than that, and more than his positional power, the stand Rev. Smith took, his support and affirmation were deeply appreciated, as well as a model to others. Hierarchical structures of the church are often unjust and need reform. The saying, "the master's tools cannot dismantle the master's house," is still true. Yet to bring about change in a timely fashion often requires that we work with those in power. Kelly Brown Douglas points out that "prudent use of the master's tools" may help us understand the "subtleties of the master's house." Using Michael Foucault's analysis of power, she concludes that change begins with altering patterns of power in interpersonal relationships.[12] Making enemies often goes with the territory of change, but you need friends. The strategy within the Christian community, it seems, ought to be to try to make friends rather than enemies.

There is a sentiment in some business circles that if change is going to occur, those at the top have to support it, yet those at the top often resist change because they want to keep the status quo (that got them to the top) intact. Many of the new humanitarian organizations and corporations have induced effective change when those in powerful positions recognize that change is needed, as with Rev. Smith. Yet change does not come by way of the top down. When we stop looking at organizations as ladders or pyramids and start seeing them as connections of relationships, we understand that change moves in mysterious ways through an organization. Barbara Kellerman, executive director of the Center for Public Leadership at Harvard's John F. Kennedy School of Government, points out that real change is often generated by people outside the system.[13] Organizations such as the British Methodist Women's Forum operated outside of church structure for years to give women a voice. We are not solely dependent on those in the system for change.

Back talk means that we ought to be in conversation, even with those we think are against us. Whenever we believe we have all the answers, we find ourselves in *mitzrayim,* the Hebrew word for Egypt, which means narrow, confining places. Whenever we shut out the possibility of learning from our adversary, we are trapped in mitzrayim; we are in exile. Respected leaders can help us make small gains that add up to big change. This does not need to be exploitation or manipulation, but recognition that others can help us achieve a greater good. In a culture that is mesmerized each week with reality TV, this strategy may be misunderstood. Shows like *Survivor* and *The Apprentice* involve making manipulative alliances in order to get people voted off the island or fired.

Choosing up sides is not only unhealthy, it is increasingly more difficult in an ambiguous world, and "voting people off the island" is not an activity that seems to be in keeping with the Christian faith. Alliances may be for inclusion rather than exclusion and for strengthening the church in positive ways. This being said, there are limits to working within the system. In several other cases, notably in the Episcopal Church, proponents of women's ordination received poor tactical advice from leaders in the church, which delayed progress. Sometimes there comes a time when the system or leaders within the system cannot help you. We have to wisely discern when that time comes.

How One Woman Changed Understandings of Church

Rev. Elsa Florez is currently engaged in a promising ministry with the Hispanic community in a large northeastern city. It has been a hard-fought battle, however. Elsa was a teacher and social worker in Puerto Rico. She came to the U.S. for further study and became involved in a suburban congregation. Soon she began using her teaching skills to lead a Bible study in Spanish. She learned how to look to the community for services to help immigrants. Her work with immigrants caused some friction in the congregation. Some people murmured, "Is she helping illegals?" "Is she trying to bring in *those* people?" "Why don't they learn to speak English?" Still, her pastor recognized her gifts for ministry and encouraged her to go to seminary. Elsa could not help but wonder if the pastor really saw those gifts or if he was just trying to get rid of her! Nevertheless, she came to grips with the fact that God was calling her.

The ordination process was difficult for Elsa. She was assigned to a mentor who was not encouraging. The mentor was a woman who thought that Elsa would have too tough of a time in ministry because she was a divorced, Hispanic woman. When she took the psychological test for ministry, she was told by the psychologist that because she was from another culture, she might have problems in ministry. When she went before the board of ordination, she was asked questions like, "Do you hate men because of your divorce?" She was told to try to tone down her accent so people could understand her. When she tried to address the issues, they told her she was being defensive. She was rejected two years in a row. She believes it was, in part, because she told the ordaining board that she was called to ministry with immigrants, a specialized ministry. They would have no place to send her. Meanwhile she continued in seminary, became interested in campus ministry, and had an opportunity to be involved in an outreach to Hispanics in a large university system. About her third try for ordination she says, "I guess they realized I wasn't giving up." A summer study opportunity in a program for Hispanic seminarians helped her discern that her call was to Hispanic ministry. But she was told by her conference that an appointment to Hispanic ministry was not possible.

Again, she did not give up. In a community with a growing Hispanic population, she went to church after church armed with demographic statistics, asking for space for a Hispanic ministry. Seven churches rejected her. Finally, one said yes. A new mission church established as a ministry with the poor with a compassionate pastor agreed to the project. She found that the ministry began with her serving as a mediator with the people. She used what she learned about the community. She received some grants to help her get started and to pay her salary. She began a tutoring program. "It was difficult for the conference to see that what I was doing was a legitimate clergy appointment," she explained. Because she did not have many people in Sunday morning worship at first—usually ten to twenty people, it was not considered a church, but a mission. During the week, however, she was involved in helping people with language skills and with negotiating immigration legalities, tutoring and housing issues, as well as hosting community events, conducting funerals and weddings and the like. There were other hurdles, such as conflict over space in the church. She recalled fights and hurtful exchanges over using someone's stash of candles, taking out the trash, the "most trivial of the trivial."

I asked Elsa how she stood all that rejection. She said she learned to deal with her anger and practice forgiveness. She learned that what she thought were trivial concerns uncovered deeper resentments and fears that require the antidote of love. She knew she was called by God, so she willed herself to hold on and pray. Eventually, the district and conference came to recognize her ministry as a legitimate appointment and as a church. Recently her ministry was honored in her conference and held up as a model for the church's crosscultural ministry. She is now often called in as an expert on how to start new churches!

Strategy #3: Stick It Out with Chutzpa

I asked her what she did to change their minds. Did the mission have a sudden growth spurt? "Not a big one," she replied. "We still have unpredictable attendance. I think it was really two things. One was I stuck it out. They figured out I wasn't going anywhere. I'm a cancer survivor, you know." Elsa thought and added in answer to my question, "The other thing I did was I proved myself. I did my homework and I persuaded the hierarchy that my call and my ministry were indeed church, even if it may not look like what they thought of as church. I got my theological rationales together and I took them to the conference office," she joked. Elsa provides a good lesson. Often when we face failure or rejection, we leave. Like the woman pastor mentioned in a previous chapter, if we feel we are in a no-win situation, we give up or go on to something else. One can hardly fail to understand why she left, but Elsa's story suggests an alternative strategy.

Change does not come quickly or easily and most times not without pain. Elsa had faith. She did not need fame or recognition; she just wanted to be in ministry and firmly believed that the church would affirm her gifts. "I have what my Jewish friend calls *chutzpa*," Elsa laughed. It is a kind of imaginative persistence that after awhile people cannot ignore. "It is something that I think is needed for ministry these days," she said. It should be said that some associate the keep-a-stiff-upper-lip approach to change with a male patriarchal model. The stoic notion of "hang in there" and suppress the pain and hurt and wait it out can be unhealthy. This strategy, however comes with chutzpa! It does not encourage people to deny or mask their anger or pain—just the opposite. We stick it out, but we don't fade quietly into the woodwork.

First, a movie from awhile back about a pig named Babe provides illustration. *Babe* is the story of how a farmer believed he could train a pig to become a sheepherder. The connotations for women in ministry are not subtle! It is the story about a species doing something that species is not supposed to do, according to society's mores. A pig is not supposed to be a sheepherder—only dogs can be sheepherders. Babe came to hold her own with sheepherding dogs, which for generations had been bred for this task. The movie affirms that what you need for life and for creating change are three things: imagination, faith, and persistence.

The farmer was able to imagine a pig as a sheepherding animal, a task that in most minds is impossible. He was able to envision Babe doing what sheep-herding dogs do. Secondly, he had faith that Babe could do it. Despite the doubt and ridicule of all those around him, it was a faith in something beyond himself that would empower Babe. Moreover, he and Babe had persistence. They worked hard at becoming sheepherders and did not give up. Banking on faith and imagination, they practiced their art and perfected it so that the sheepherding establishment had to take notice and had to acknowledge that a pig could become a sheepherding animal. *Babe,* a movie targeted to children, captured the imaginations of adults because, for one reason, it gets at the ethos of life and leadership. With persistence, imagination, faith, and chutzpa, one can survive rejections and live into one's call.

Why a Lay Woman Crusades for Women's Ordination

Christina Rees, a devout Anglican laywoman, is by profession a freelance television and radio broadcaster and writer in England. A lifelong Christian, she is a well-known lay preacher and was elected to the General Synod, the governing body of the Church of England, in 1990. She also has edited a wonderfully inspiring book, *Voices of this Calling: Experiences of the First Generation of Women Priests.* She told me about her work with the Movement for the Ordination of Women (MOW) and how they campaigned to get the Church of England to change its mind.

For many years she has had a vision of the church in which women are equally valued—the vision of Galations 3:28: "There is no longer Jew or Greek, there is no longer slave or free, there is no longer male and female; for all of you are one in Christ Jesus." Christina said, "I believe that the core message of the gospel is forgiveness, liberation in Christ Jesus and unity in the Spirit. In the kingdom of God men and women are valued equally, and I believe that vision can and should come to pass in the present."

In chapter three I noted how the Church of England voted on November 11, 1992, to ordain women. Christina Rees recalled that day in the Assembly Hall in Church House, Westminster. "There was a tense hush as the Archbishop of Canterbury at that time read the results." All three bodies—the House of Bishops, the House of Clergy, and the House of Laity—voted in favor of the measure. There was silence. In a press gallery someone squeaked, then a squeal went up. People burst into tears and cheered. History had been made. One male vicar wrote of his memory of the aftermath of the 1992 vote:

[O]ne thing impressed me more than any other. Not the cheering and singing outside Church House, but the way in which many ordinary people, many of whom had not darkened a church for years, would stop me in the street and tell me how pleased they were. The Church had done something which the Decade of Evangelism had singularly failed to do. It had caught the public imagination. They felt caught up in what had happened. Like Berlin and South Africa, another wall had fallen.[14]

Though denied ordination for many years and still denied in some traditions, several women that I interviewed talked about being priests anyway. One woman wrote, "I have been a common law priest for twenty-five years, and I just want the church to make an honest woman of me."[15] The affirmative vote did not come easy. Though Christina Rees was thrilled that hard work paid off, she shared with me her ongoing pain over a grudging attitude toward women in the church. Many have embraced women priests, but still many others take the attitude, "Well, okay, if we have to." She says, "Patriarchy is the hardest thing to die. What should be self-evident, it seems to me, women as equal partners in ministry, is amazingly resisted."

Her hunch has been documented by Mark Chaves, whose study found that prior to 1920 there was little organized opposition to women's ordination. Organized opposition increased from 1920 to 1970 and again increased in denominational conflicts regarding ordination after 1970. So given the gains made by women and the move toward gender equality in all segments of society, one might expect the opposition to lessen. In fact, the opposite is true.[16] Christina Rees testified that great amounts of energy are expended in keeping the tradition of patriarchy alive. She cited two examples:

After the vote, the Church of England paid out over 26 million pounds in "financial provisions" to 450 male priests who left the church because of the decision to ordain women. Some of those men claimed that it was no longer the church they were ordained in and asked to be released because they could not, would not serve with women. Some became Roman Catholic priests. Some, ironically, joined other denominations who already ordained women, such as the Methodists. Christina told me that seventy of those have come back, thirty have taken up paid positions, and only one has paid the money back. Another example was the passing of the Act of Synod almost one year exactly after the vote on women priests. The act allowed for "the creation of a new kind of ecclesiastical creature—the flying bishop" (known officially as Provincial Episcopal Visitors, or PEVs). This meant that some parishes who opposed women's ordination could come under a PEV and be protected against having a woman priest or even a male bishop come to celebrate who had laid hands on a woman to ordain her. So there is still a need for vigilance. The goals of MOW were accomplished, so a new group, Women and the Church (WATCH), was formed. This group is working toward the effort to permit women bishops in the Church of England. Ecumenical talks with British Methodists have been held up because of the Church of England's resistance to women bishops. There is also a coalition, the Group for Rescinding the Act of Synod (GRAS), working to eliminate the possibility of opting out of getting a woman priest.

I asked Christina why a laywoman would care so much or work so hard for women's ordination. It is a question she is frequently asked. In many ways it is the wrong question. Why wouldn't she care? First of all, Christina says, "I did not want people to think I was doing it for me." She campaigned for women's ordination not for her own benefit, but because she believed so strongly in the theological reasons for doing it. Second, she does not, at this time, perceive her call to be to the priesthood. She believes she received the gift of preaching at age seventeen and has several advanced theological degrees, but she believes she can best fulfill her call as a lay person. AMEN! It also ensures that she is freer to speak out on some issues. "Where a woman priest may feel compelled to 'let it go,' I can voice objections to discriminatory practices." We could use a few clones of Christina Rees!

Strategy #4: Create a Coalition

Christina Rees talked about the mounting resistance prior to the 1992 vote to ordain women, which MOW responded to with more campaigning. They wrote letters, conducted workshops in churches on why women priests were a good thing, talked with neighbors, and spoke with the media. The campaign intensified from July to November. She and others in MOW became aware that they were fourteen votes shy. "Our mission was to change the minds of fourteen people." They identified those who were most likely to change their minds, wrote them, had lunch with them, debated with them. Christina told me, "I did not know for sure if we had the votes, but I was given a kind of divine assurance two weeks before the vote, or I would not just have bitten my nails, I would have bitten my fingers off!"

Rev. Kenny Smith used a bottom-up approach to leading change, working with others to move through the tension involving women in ministry. Shunning the limelight, he invited women into the sessions to teach and preach so that it seemed natural. He recognized that change has to be led by individuals throughout an organization. John Kotter says that gathering a coalition and deploying people is an effective way to energize change. A dictatorial leader that demands change may get it, but usually it turns out to be change for the worse. It may serve to strengthen resistance and put up more barriers to change. Many who have been through difficult and unsuccessful change efforts come away feeling angry and cynical. They are reluctant to support any kind of change effort again. Kotter says that failing to create a "sufficiently powerful guiding coalition" is one of the crucial errors that may cause failure to bring about change.[17]

Leaders empowered by the people tend to be agents of change. Again, this is not creating manipulative, *Survivor* alliances, but a community of people who care about one another and their organization. A coalition does not have to be a cast of thousands, but there is strength in a critical mass. A few good dedicated people whom you nurture and whose gifts you affirm can bring forth tremendous results. Kotter warns against two kinds of individuals in creating a coalition—those with super huge egos and the "snakes," those who create mistrust by telling Lou something about Sara and telling Sara something about Lou. Each of these, Kotter says, will contribute about as much as "nuclear waste."[18] Building a coalition is nothing new. It is done all the time in community organizing, but we often fail to do it and then wonder why we can't bring about change in our churches. Some conclude that aging churches are unable to change and that we must accept that. Others disagree; they have led and seen change.

"Never underestimate the power of people when you gather them together and use their gifts," says Christina Rees. Connecting with people is, again, not to manipulate or use them, but to gain from their presence. While sheer numbers themselves do not create change, they can enhance the possibility for change. More women claimed their call to ministry, which caused people to rethink their reasons for excluding them.

Strategy #5: Do Your Homework: Engage in Theological Reflection

Christina Rees says that even though she had a conviction that women's ordination was the right thing to do, she asked herself about the theological basis for this change. Why would centuries of church tradition need to change? She also had a sense that God called her to hold up that theological rationale and to hold the church accountable to it. Theological reflection on the experience of oppression of women and how the Christian faith responds or should respond is crucial, as she explains: "I truly believe in the radical mutuality of the Gospel, a dynamic of love that says we are all created in God's image, and that God loves us equally, that there is no hierarchy in the Godhead and that is how we are to treat each other."[19] This kind of theological reflection helps us to form a positive vision. It is one thing to complain about something, but you'd better come in with something better. Know why you want change; otherwise it appears that we are just jumping on somebody's bandwagon. In terms of her own involvement in the struggle, Christina asked herself, "What will happen if I do nothing?" Though she realized that the movement would have continued, ultimately she knew she had to act on her faith commitment. She joined with others who also wrestled with the theological issues. She concludes that because of their deep convictions and serious reflection, those working for ordination were able to communicate their vision effectively. As Jean Miller Schmidt has written, "The power to transform the world must be rooted in profound spirituality, biblical faith and theological reflection (and not simply human effort) while insisting equally that this must not mean conforming to a particular type of piety."[20]

Several Korean women I spoke with talked about how *minjung* theology has guided them. It is a theology born out of solidarity and mutuality with the poor and exploited. They talked about the experience of Third World women (and children) sweatshop laborers, about the division of their country into North and South, the oppressive governments. Minjung is a Korean term consisting of two Chinese characters meaning "the common people or masses who are subjugated or ruled."[21] "This is how many of us endured," one woman said, "by supporting each other, by envisioning a better world." In Korea, women's ordination was continually voted down until 1995 when finally that door was opened. In "God Weeps with Our Pain," Kwok Pui-lan writes: "Feminist theology in Asia is not written with a pen, it is inscribed on the hearts of many who feel the pain, and yet dare to hope."[22]

The resistance to change was and is stalwart. That resistance can take on beastly proportions. Know what you are getting into—it can get ugly, one woman advised. Theological reflection and action, otherwise known as praxis, is not for the faint of heart. One has to be prepared to convince the inconvincable, forging, not forcing, change out of well-thought-out beliefs.

From Farm Girl to District Superintendent

Rita Callis talked openly with me about some of her experiences in ministry in The United Methodist Church. She has many wonderful insights, a great sense of humor, and conveys a deep wisdom. She recounted the story of her call. Rita was raised on a farm, one of seven children. Without a clear sense of direction in her life, and no opportunity to go to college, she decided to go to beauty school. This being in the day of the flower child, Rita had never worn make-up or done much with her hair. "Whatever made me think I could be a beautician, I'll never know," she said. "But one particular day at beauty school we practiced doing 'up-dos' on each other. That evening I went to a revival service at my church with the biggest Bee Hive you've ever seen." Previously Rita had some glimpses of the call to ministry in her life. Her pastor had taken her all-white youth group to visit an all-black church where she heard a woman preach for the first time. It was Leontine Kelly, who was then serving as pastor at that church. (She later became a bishop.) "Along with my pastor, Leontine Kelly, my new mentor, began to encourage me to listen for God's call to preach." But that evening, during the revival service, she realized that God wanted her to go into the ministry. During the altar call Rita went forward along with others who responded to the preacher's invitation. "If you feel God has something more for your life, come now." She went forward, big hair and all. As the preacher and her pastor began laying hands on those kneeling at the altar, Rita knew this was a really important turning point in her life. But at that moment all she could think about was, "Is this going to take through all this hair?" Well, it did indeed "take," and college and seminary came next. After college and seminary she recalls getting a bank loan to buy a motorcycle to get her around the countryside where her appointment was. The bank president, a good Baptist, was quick to approve the loan, "Why

Rev. Callis, you could even take this off your taxes. It is a great evangelism tool. You could give your church folks a ride on your new motorcycle and scare the hell out of them one soul at a time."

When she first started out in the early eighties, things were rocky. She was asked to go to a church in another area. When she met her supervisor (the district superintendent) for the first time, he informed her that when the church learned they were getting a woman pastor, they cut the salary, hoping that would keep her from coming. He said to her, "Your previous superintendent said you were so wonderful. He didn't bother to mention you've been divorced. Count yourself lucky to come to my district, and I don't want to hear anything about this salary business." It didn't occur to Rita that she wouldn't go. This was to be her appointment. So she went and bloomed where she had been planted. She says all she did was "Be who I was and claim my call." She became good friends with one of the church matriarchs. At a later charge conference meeting this woman spoke, "I was one of the ones most opposed to a 'lady preacher' but this one has made me eat my words. I think God sent her here to us." The woman then recommended that they restore Rita's salary to what it was, and the church voted to do so right in the presence of the district superintendent (D.S.), who had scolded her.

Four years ago Rita was asked by her bishop to serve as a district superintendent. She didn't want to do it. She confessed a dislike for church hierarchy. "I never did the political thing—just kept my nose clean, stayed out of it. Besides, my new husband and I had gotten married just a few years earlier, and this meant we would have to live apart." After much prayer, however, Rita accepted, coming to the realization that God could use her in that position, that she could make a difference. "And if women kept saying no, they would quit being asked," she said.

"There have been dark days for me in ministry," Rita confided. "Mostly over the pain of being divorced, single and lonely." She has served some "dysfunctional, ingrown" churches. She learned to operate out of her gut instinct, to build relationships and extend on those. She learned to accept people or a congregation where they are and then build a bridge. She acknowledges that women still have a long way to go in gaining acceptance. As a district superintendent, she saw some churches write on their ministry profile, "Do not send us a woman." She replies, "I don't think women graduating from seminary are prepared for that." She reminds herself that "this is what God has called me to do." As her pastor advised from the beginning, "If there is anything else in the world that you can do other than go into the ministry, then you ought to do it. But if this is what God has called you to do, you won't be able to do anything else."

"I just feel privileged that God has called me into that sacred space in people's lives," Rita said. "People need to believe that the pastor is genuinely concerned about them. You gotta' love 'em. I count it a lifetime of honor to be able to do that."

Strategy #6: Have a Sense of Humor and Use It

When nothing else was going well or seemed to work, Rita dug deep and called upon her sense of humor. As Voltaire once said, "O Lord, make my enemies ridiculous." Rita also believes that people in ministry have to be able to laugh at themselves, that it is a great sign of strength not to fear that acknowledging one's humanness can take away one's power. She tells stories on herself that break barriers. For instance, she relayed to me how she was trying to recruit a very promising clergywoman candidate to come to her district.

> I met Amy at the nicest restaurant in the area. She was very sharp, a graduate of a well-respected seminary and very personable. I had several appointments I needed to fill. I was telling Amy about how, yes, this was a rural area, but that there was a lot of culture, festivals, concerts, etc. About that time a patron of the restaurant went over and plunked in his quarters in the jukebox. Just at the moment I was about to convince Amy of the charms of the community came blasting from the jukebox that ole' redneck national anthem, "Let's Get Drunk and _____." We looked at each other and exploded into laughter. So much for culture.

Amy still came to Rita's district to serve. That sense of humor has also helped her as she was one of only two clergywomen on the cabinet of district superintendents. She does not see this as being "one of the boys." She has learned to be comfortable with her sexuality and who she is, being outrageous at times by her own admission. She recalls one cabinet meeting with the bishop and all the other superintendents, except the one other woman superintendent was not there. During a break, they all went out, and just outside their meeting room were two restrooms, one for men and one for women. She waltzed in the women's while the men lined up to use the men's room. When she came out, she told them, "Why don't you do like we women do at concerts? We use the men's room and stand watch for each other." They took her advice. Later that day, Rita had to "go" again, so she excused herself from the meeting. She went in the women's room and fell in. She told me how she stormed back into the meeting and declared, "If you are going to use the women's room, at least put the seat down!" The men all howled with laughter. She affirmed her gender and talked back through humor.

When I was in London doing research for this book, I came back to my hotel after a long day and absent-mindedly switched on the TV just to see what was on British television. I had not had the TV on before this. Serendipitously, a sitcom about a single woman vicar was in progress. The premise of the show was that a woman, kind of a quick-witted Rosie O'Donnell, was vicar of a small village parish, and her parishioners were, at various levels, dysfunctional. The show was uproariously funny and humane. The main character was down-to-earth, patient, and a regular person with pictures of Jesus and Brad Pitt on her wall. I asked one of the clergywomen I interviewed the next day about the show. She told me that the show is called "The Vicar of Dibley," and that it is a huge hit in Britain. She claimed that the woman vicar is actually a decent role model. The Vicar of Dibley is sure about her call, relates well to the people, empathizes with them, and stirs them out of their complacent faith. And she's just funny. On the first show of the television series, when she first arrived in Dibley, she met the only four active parishioners and responded to their shock at their new vicar being a woman: "You were expecting a bloke with a beard and bad breath, carrying a Bible. What you got is a babe with a bob and beautiful bosoms!" The Vicar of Dibley keeps her cool and her perspective throughout the ups and downs of parish life. Her humor is saving grace. Male clergy, by contrast, have been depicted in the media as uptight, weak, and sniveling. One clergywoman I interviewed takes it in stride when she walks down the street in London wearing her collar and construction workers call out, "Hey, Vicar of Dibley!"

There are times, of course, when humor is not appropriate and can serve to undermine women and cause them not to be taken seriously. According to Marjorie Procter-Smith, humor can be used to trivialize or dismiss legitimate concerns, and it has often been used by men to dominate, hence one comes up against the limits of this strategy.[23] Rita, however, feels that her opinions are valued and sought after because she can laugh at herself without demeaning or diminishing herself. "Humor, used properly, is a language that builds bridges," she reflects. She sees back talk not as polemical or moralizing, but as a way of learning from experience and drawing wisdom from sharing stories. It helped her to build relationships that allowed her to create change where she served, including the cabinet. Though unpretentious, Rita had a role in bringing a different approach to the appointment process in her district which the bishop supported. Instead of the usual "insider trading," she advocated looking at the people's gifts and the needs of congregations. Many leaders I spoke with agree with the need to maintain perspective and a sense of humor during times of crisis, and pointed to the underrated sense of humor of Jesus. Humor acknowledges our humanity, and it is a way forward, a way of change.

Strategy #7: Be Clear About Your Call, About Who You Are and What Gifts You Bring

"What helped me in my churches," Rita says, "is that people could sense that I was authentic—that I cared about them and wanted to be their pastor. Relationships are what make the difference. For example, one of my gifts is front-porch sitting. We ought to have a seminary course in front-porch sitting. Too many pastors just don't know how to listen and be with people. We are all so busy and hell bent on getting things done. People in my churches appreciate the fact that I would take time with them."

When I asked Rita what she did in her churches to bring about change, she talked about how she had served one church that was very, very ingrown, that did not accept outsiders, and that voiced the harsh judgment, "Preachers come and go, but this is *our* church." In other words, you are just the hired help. Sometimes a church like this has to hit rock bottom and in the crisis will start to ask what really is our mission here, what are we about. "That is very healthy," Rita says. "In this process they find out who I am, I find out who they are, and we go from there."

Rita clarified, "When you have a church like this, I say you've got to have a few good funerals." She explained that she did not intend to be insensitive, but she means this in two ways. First, if some strong people in a congregation like this die and you offer good pastoral care to the families and a few well-planned and preached funerals where the people are honored, then the survivors and the church members really come to appreciate you. You've earned their respect and loyalty. In the second sense, a few good funerals also means that change is possible, that previous ways of doing things may have died when the proponents of these ways entered into the resurrected life. Obviously, leaders cannot go killing off those who get in their way. But death is part of God's plan for making way for the new. This does not diminish our appreciation for the saints, but with each of those funerals some of the resistance to change dies, too. This is part of what John Kotter means when he advises leaders to move away from structures, systems, or patterns of behavior that block or undermine change. People who are in power for long periods of time often have institutionalized structures that can prevent improvement.

A leader can sometimes delicately allow those structures to come to a natural demise. If those obstacles cannot be removed, work around them or wait them out while empowering others to implement change.[24]

"When you claim your call, you can always fall back on that," Rita says. "You know that you are here for a reason. Then you just follow your instincts and do what needs to be done. Most people would recognize and appreciate my gifts once they got to know me. We don't need to be imposters." She does acknowledge that the church has a way of stifling the gifts of some. Elsa experienced that, but she exercised this strategy and stuck it out. Rena Yocum calls this "ungifting." Women often have the experience of the church denying or not valuing who they are and what they bring. Yocum said, "Our gifts are deemed undesirable because they do not match the ecclesial furniture or because they are not like anything anybody has envisioned."[25]

Women from some traditions that do not ordain them have been known to downplay their competence. For example, pentecostal women may claim incompetence or say they have no merit on their own, but just have to get up and preach anyway due to an irresistible call from God or moving of the Spirit.[26] Women should not have to put themselves down to fulfill their call, nor is claiming one's call about arrogance or egotism, but about centering on Jesus Christ. We can teach and preach to the church so that it affirms the leadership gifts and styles of women. We have a long way to go. In the meantime, a good strategy is to continue to receive encouragement from confidence in the call to ministry.

Gifts that women bring are increasingly valued and, as John Matthews claims, men with these gifts that are so needed now may feel that they can put them into practice, whereas they may have stifled them before because they were not as valued. Claiming one's call and gifts is a way of talking back to resistance, of refusing to let it dampen the spirit.

How a Deacon Rescued a Shelter

Marjorie Baker, a deacon in the Midwest, was hired in 1998 by the area's Council of Churches to direct the community's homeless shelter and food bank. Marjorie had a background in social work and had formerly directed a housing program in another state. She was to be in charge of day-to-day operations of the facilities. The Council of Churches was the governing board and began the shelter in the 1980s, when homelessness in the community was at its peak.

Marjorie had some new ideas for expanding services, including job training and counseling, which was a particular passion of hers. She shared some of her ideas at her interview. Little did she know when she came on board that the community shelter was nearly bankrupt and was within a few months of closing. She asked about the finances of the shelter at her interview and was assured that the treasurer, who was on the council, had everything under control. The two employees, former clients of the shelter, were oblivious to the financial situation. Marjorie discovered the problem only after she pressed for information at her first council meeting as director. "Why didn't you tell me?" she asked. "At least I would have known what I was getting into." The council claimed that they did not know the extent of the problem, but admitted they did not think the shelter would survive. They hired Marjorie partly because they thought she might salvage it, but partly because it was just expected of them.

The books were kept by a woman member of the council who was also the longtime treasurer of her local church. Initially, Marjorie was glad to have someone else handle the money. Naturally she was alarmed to learn the true financial picture. She found she could probably keep the shelter going for about six months with the current financial resources without any expansion of services, only paying salaries and bills. Marjorie was distraught and felt betrayed. She thought about quitting and moving on, but she decided to stick it out and accept the challenge. "It is the deacon in me, I guess. I am just called to this ministry," she said. "Someone told me once that in Spanish, the word deacon means 'one who helps your heart get larger.' That is what I want to do—expand people's hearts. God was just telling me to stay. I had my bags packed several times, but just could not get out the door." Deacons have been described as "rescuers," not in the co-dependent sense of trying to fix everything or bringing home every stray puppy, but in the sense of observing a need and gathering the resources needed to respond to it.

Marjorie went to the next council meeting and confronted the members with the reality of the situation. They confirmed it was grim. The loss of the only community shelter would mean that an increasing population of unemployed persons in the area would have to seek help from individual churches or have no where to turn at all. "In many ways it was a case of classic denial. I think they could not take any action because that would mean admitting there was a problem."

Marjorie assessed the assets of the shelter. There were faithful volunteers, two good employees, an adequate facility that needed some repair, a good location, and a good reputation in the community. She asked the clients what the shelter meant for them. She imagined what the shelter could be like, what further help it could provide for the community. She set up an advisory committee of clients and past clients of the shelter, listened to them, and consulted with them for ways to bring about hope to marginalized people in the community.

She asked the Council of Churches to find ways to raise money. The response dismayed her: "We can't ask people for more money." She got the impression that they did not really want to save the shelter. She became aware of the theological and philosophical differences on the council. Being an ecumenical group, this was not unexpected, but Marjorie saw how these differences were dividing the group and harming the shelter. The woman who held the purse strings even said at one meeting, "Those people should just go out and get a job." Marjorie was confounded as to why such a person would want to serve on the Council of Churches anyway. Still, even others on the council expressed little enthusiasm for revitalizing the shelter. "The feeling seemed to be that homelessness was less of a problem now with economic prosperity," Marjorie confided. "I had to convince them that there are still homeless people and they need help and that the church has a mandate to feed the hungry, clothe the naked, and take care of those in need."

Was the desire to help others in the community waning? Marjorie needed to know. Without the support of the council, there was little hope for the shelter. She began to talk to people and ask questions. She found among most a sincere desire to continue the ministry but always complete confusion about how to do it. She decided to come up with a plan to present to the council. She thought it might cause conflict and even more dissension, but it was a risk she had to take.

She had begun to do some research into available grants. She was pleased by what she discovered. Her plan had four strategies for action:

1. She would apply for grants.

2. She would look to the people closest by for help—those right around her. She would go to churches, talk about the ministry and the volunteers, and how the shelter has helped people and the community. She would ask people to join her in her efforts. She would create a video to communicate their mission.

3. She and her advisory committee would go to the community. She would contact businesses, community organizations, police and fire authorities, anyone who might have a stake in keeping the shelter alive.

4. The shelter would expand services. She would invite the homeless and formerly homeless to participate in discussions and decision making about needed services. She would hire a job counselor and hold job-training classes, including resume development, and operate a child-care facility.

Before she took the plan to the council she decided to run it by a few of the members first. She was fearful that the naysayers on the council would kill the plan before it had a chance. She called five key council members and set up individual lunch dates with each of them. She explained her plan and listened to their suggestions about what other groups she might invite into the process, who had experience with grant writing, etc. She asked for their support for her plan. Some of them warned her of who the nemeses would be on the council, who had a stake in the status quo. She prepared to face them.

She went to the council with her plan. She hoped it would turn around their thinking and get them to brainstorm about other possibilities. She was on the agenda for the evening, but the chair put her near the end. "The male chairperson had a way of blowing me off. This was one of them, making me the last priority of the council." She relayed how he would often take a pot shot or use humor as a put down. "He was a master of the put-you-in-your-place quip." Marjorie felt tears well up. She could have responded in kind but decided not to stoop to that level. Nor would she cower in a corner. She would learn to talk back. She engaged the group in some serious theological reflection that refuted the notion that caring for the homeless is optional—a nice thing to do if you've got the money. She asked some probing questions: "Are you ready to open up your church or the guest room in your house to the homeless? What did you start this ministry for anyway if you were going to let it die? Why exactly are you willing to abandon the homeless of our community?"

Marjorie made her plea and explained her plan. Several members looked down at their papers avoiding eye contact with her. Several pursed their lips in disapproval. When she finished, one of the members she had lunch with spoke in support. Another, a woman rector from the Episcopal Church, responded enthusiastically, "This is a wonderful plan. We need to do this." A few objections were raised, but they did not gain much steam. The treasurer was baffled but remained quiet. One by one, Marjorie addressed them calmly, but firmly. The main objection had been begging for money from churches. She explained that the shelter is not something other than the church, but an extension of the ministry of the church. The council voted to support Marjorie's plan.

She and her colleagues immediately set to work on her plan. Grant writing was tedious work, but with the help of a community volunteer, she was able to procure almost immediately three small grants amounting to $26,000. It was a start. She went to denominational heads for assistance. Three members of the council met regularly with her. One of these began work on the video, which she took to local churches and businesses and community events. A local insurance company volunteered to insure them at substantial savings.

Each time she met with the council, Marjorie seemed to have more and more respect and support. They saw how she mobilized others for change. Two of the "old guard" retired and two new people came to the council. Today the community shelter is thriving and has expanded, offering child care and job training. The shelter has developed relationships with other community organizations and businesses. Marjorie told me her story not because she wanted to brag about her accomplishments and how she blew through the crisis, but because I convinced her that others would benefit from her witness.

Strategy #8: Lobby for Change

To many the word "lobby" is a bad word conjuring up corrupt "Washington types" or special interest groups on Capitol Hill buying votes. Marjorie wisely shared her plan with a few people and tested the waters of the council. She recalls, "If those initial people had told me to forget it, I would have. But they gave me hope. When I had their support, I felt I could gain more." She did not go in and just dictate what she wanted to do. "I did not have enough respect yet. I had not gained their trust." This is not a "divide and conquer" strategy, but a networking one. Marjorie did not so much ask council members to choose sides; she asked them what they thought, and she listened to them. She garnered support before going in simply by asking the right people. In contrast, one male pastor newly appointed to a large church went to a church vestry meeting with a proposal to spend money to build a parking lot. He seemed to expect people to go along with him simply because he said they should, on the basis of his positional authority. He shunned the need to garner support for his idea, putting too much stock in his own charisma. When they did not just go along, he lost interest in the church. He claimed they were a dying congregation who, because they did not support him, was a lost cause.

I asked a group of clergywomen about lobbying for change. "Knowing how to lobby is critical in ministry," said one. "I don't see it as a political or manipulative thing. It is just planting seeds of change—throwing out an idea and seeing if it takes root." Christina Rees told me about how the Movement for the Ordination of Women lobbied for the fourteen votes they needed to get the Church of England to pass legislation affirming women's ordination. Another woman voiced her view: "I've seen it be abused, though. I've seen people line up their 'forces' against someone or some issue. It can be mean-spirited." Still most of the church leaders I spoke with saw the need for persistent discussion and wrestling with questions and challenges facing the church to instigate needed change.

Many or even most leadership strategies can be abused if conducted for self-serving purposes. When personal ambition enters into a person's ministry, "it festers and spreads like a skin disease. It becomes uncontrollable and takes over one's life. Pretty soon that's all you think about," confessed one clergywoman. Back talk, nevertheless, is sometimes talk to convince or raise consciousness. It is sometimes like the widow before the judge in Jesus' parable in Luke 18:1–8. Back talk is not one person demanding allegiance and top-down change, but it recognizes that change comes out of continued conversation and dialogue. Christina Rees insists they would not buy votes or advocate exploitative factions, but used the power of words to persuade people of the gospel call to justice.

How a Vicar's Underwear Stands for Change

I spoke with a very wise woman in England who pastors a church in a small village. She generously shared her wonderful, sometimes hilarious, sometimes incredulous stories of being a part of the first group of women ordained in her tradition. She and the other women in her class were told they were to wear long-sleeve straight frocks with a white collar and no make-up. They posed for a picture, which she still has, all lined up looking identical and sexless in their straight black dresses and sensible shoes. Little did the authorities know that the women decided to rebel in their own way. They decided to rebel quietly, so as not to jeopardize the possibility that they would be able to fulfill their call to ministry. The women had agreed that under those ugly, frumpy frocks, they would all wear bright red, sexy underwear! The bishops must be wondering to this day why the women were all grinning so big in that picture. It was a way that they could remain true to themselves on the inside, even while it was necessary (in those days, anyway) to conform on the outside to the standards that the males had set for them. Now red underwear has become a symbol for those clergywomen, a symbol of their sacrifice for their call, but also a symbol of not giving up their womanhood all together.

This story raises the issue and role of sexuality in ministry. Rather than covering up or disguising our sexuality, women are beginning to be able to celebrate it. Rita Callis remarked, "I think as women ministers, our sexuality is more out there, more obvious." She explained, "When we put on that robe, it doesn't cover up the fact that we are women. Oh, we used to try to by wearing those huge black robes that swallowed us, but even so, many of us couldn't hide!" We are sexual beings and we are coming to learn it is okay to be who we are. Rosemary Lain-Priestley, a Church of England priest since 1997, is the first female associate vicar at St. Martin-In-The-Fields in London. She has a two-year-old daughter and is pregnant with her second child. She knows that only a few years ago this would have been unheard of. The family commitments of priests were not so visible, nor were the complexities brought by their sexuality. Lain-Priestley recalled the notion—one that is still with us—that the altar has to be kept pure. Rosemary Ruether has noted that "the mother is the icon of the corruptible nature."[26] Rev. Lain-Priestley claims to bring her experience of motherhood into her preaching, but feels she can speak to both men and women. There is an old saying, "The hand that rocks the cradle should also rock the boat!" Rev. Lain-Priestley's recent advent sermon was titled "Waiting to be Born." She recalls, "I feared it would offend or be controversial, but so far I've only heard positive things." Keeping balance in her life is an ongoing struggle, but she believes that women's presence in the priesthood has freed men also to claim the need for balance.

The "red-underwear clergywomen" in that first group of female clergy serve as role models and mentors for a new breed of women clerics in England. "They can now be proud of their sexuality," one woman rejoiced. These women shared with me stories of their acceptance in their parishes. "Most of our village churches love women pastors," one shared, "because we care for them. We are not aloof, only concerned with the sermon or the communion wine. We love and care for our sheep, and the people respond to that." Another ventured, "I think people realize that it is *precisely* because we are women that we do that. Being a woman is an advantage."

The British clergywomen told me about the strong solidarity they have and how mentoring is a main source of support *and* a means of change. Although the "woman against woman" syndrome is not unheard of by them, they take great pride in their strong support system and relationships among women, clergy and lay.

Strategy #9: Mentor and Befriend Colleagues

Affirming women's leadership is a needed area of change identified in chapter two. It is needed because the church requires the gifts that women bring. Mentoring is a way of bringing that affirmation. The women pioneers in ministry, who had no role models, now serve that role. Rita Callis says that it is natural to look to other women for support and "survival strategies." Bishop Leontine Kelly was her inspiration for going into the ministry and a wonderful mentor. Men and women in ministry need mentors and role models. Rita believes that it is particularly the responsibility and privilege for experienced clergywomen to mentor those just entering the profession. One of the main reasons women leave the ministry is because of a feeling of isolation and a stuck-out-on-a-limb feeling.

Women mentoring other women flies in the face of women's inhumanity to other women. Women tell me that while they have experienced the woman-against-woman syndrome, their friendships and strong ties with other women have saved them. These bonds and community of women in ministry can indeed overcome the hurtful belief that women have to watch their backs around other women. bell hooks reminds us that we cannot change patriarchal domination when we ourselves attempt to dominate each other:

> Clearly, differentiation between strong and weak, powerful and powerless, has been a central defining aspect of gender globally, carrying with it the assumption that men should have greater authority than women, and should rule over them. As significant and important as this fact is, it should not obscure the reality that women can and do participate in politics of domination. . . . If focus on patriarchal domination masks this reality . . . then women cooperate in suppressing and promoting false consciousness, inhibiting our capacity to assume responsibility for transforming ourselves and society.[28]

It is very hypocritical for women to demand an end to patriarchal domination so they can assume leadership while at the same time getting ahead by stepping on the backs of other women. Friendship between women and mentoring is in direct opposition to this hypocrisy.

Joan Chittister wrote about the long spiritual tradition of women's friendship. Using biblical women as models, she describes how a theology of friendship derives from the understanding that God *is* friendship, and that friendship is a necessary part of the Christian life and, in particular, is indispensable for Christian leaders.[29]

Mentors teach us not to repeat their own mistakes. They lead us beyond ourselves. They encourage us when we are down and think we can go no further. They tell us the truth. Mentors do not compete with us. They do not try to fix things for us or tell us what to do. They simply are. They are those we look up to, but even as we do, they warn us not to see them as above ourselves.

Mentoring involves storytelling. It is continuing to tell the stories that give us strength. For clergywomen, we should never neglect telling the stories of hard-won gains for women, of the pioneer women who forged the way. Max DePree, noted author on leadership in business, retold a story from Nigeria relayed to him by Carl Frost to illustrate:

> Electricity had just been brought into the village where he and his family were living. Each family got a single light in its hut. A real sign of progress. The trouble was that at night, though they had nothing to read and many [villagers] did not know how to read, the families would sit in their huts in awe of this wonderful symbol of technology. The light-bulb watching began to replace the customary nighttime gatherings by the tribal fire, where the tribal storytellers, the elders, would pass along the history of the tribe. The tribe was losing its history in the light of a few electric bulbs.[30]

If we fail to tell our stories, if we engage in light bulb watching in the church, we lose our history, the values that bind us, our sense of purpose. The stories of back talk, of change must be told.

The kind of friendship a mentor offers takes all the "marshmallow," all the fluff out of human relationships. Chittister writes:

> The fact is that companionship is not enough to fill a life. What is needed in human relationships above all, if they are to give substance to our lives, is the quality of fusion, the character of meld. It is the challenge of connection. It is an insight of grave consequences in a world where we can live in crowds forever and never even notice that we are alone. It is so easy to think that we have friends and know how to be a friend when all we really have are contacts. It is so easy to think we have a relationship with someone when all we

really have is more or less time for idle conversations with people we see often but keep at a distance always.[31]

What she describes as the quality of fusion, the character of meld, and the challenge of connection is in essence back talk. It is not idle conversation but the kind of reality talk that changes us as well as helps us to bring about change.

If it seems odd to suggest that mentoring is a strategy for change, perhaps even manipulative, let me suggest that mentoring is both a means and an end, and true mentoring friendships can only further the work of the church. To mentor other women is to talk back to the notion that women can't work with other women or that women can't get along. It is to talk back to patriarchal structures that seem to benefit from women's inhumanity to other women. It is to talk back by friendship, to traverse resistance with friendship in the sign of the cross.

Strategy #10: Wear Red Underwear

Red underwear serves as a useful metaphor for not losing our identity to rules and conformity. This strategy says to do whatever it is you need to do to maintain and validate who you are in a way that is life affirming for you and those around you. I am not suggesting that we need to hide who we are under our clothes, but that fulfilling our vocation does not mean that we have to deny who we are as women. We do not need to put on an act. On the one hand we do not want our ministry to be undermined because we are too flamboyant or insensitive to what others might think. We have to strike a balance between being ourselves and fulfilling the role of minister/leader. Many people have preconceived, culturally conditioned images of what a pastor is supposed to be and look like. The presence of women in ministry has, if nothing else, challenged those. We can stretch those even further if we have their initial respect and trust.

Rev. Melissa Dunlap tells how she deliberately chose to wear a floral pink dress for her ordination. "I am tired of people thinking that clergy have to be these dour looking people." Sometimes clergywomen may be perceived to be a threat by women in their congregations. Melissa was determined to maintain her femininity. "We are after all two different genders. That pink dress was my statement that female is okay." Other people

I interviewed admitted to being more "old school" in regards to the image that women in ministry project. Sister Teresa, a deacon and priest in the Church of England, St Andrew's House, edits a newsletter, the *Distinctive News of Women in Ministry,* that serves to connect and support women church leaders internationally. She was one of the 650 women who moved from deaconess to the officially ordained diaconate. In the pressure to be accepted, some women priests acted like and dressed like men in the beginning. Now, the other extreme, she notes, is the "dangly earring gang." She objected to women serving priestly and liturgical functions wearing flashy jewelry or anything that might detract from the eucharist.

Some years ago a clergywoman friend of mine (I'll call her Fran) called me in a panic about three months into her first appointment. "Susan," she breathed frantically, "you've got to help me. I was so excited about going to _____ville to the three-point charge because I could wear my cowboy boots and jeans." Fran is a woman who has always preferred jeans and dressing down. She would not be caught dead in a pink dress. I begin to hear her sincere concern over the phone. "I need your fashion sense." Now, Fran must have been exercising the strategy of humor because I do not now, nor have I ever considered myself as someone with fashion sense. I laughed out loud, but she was serious. "I wore my jeans when I went out visitin' people. Went out in the fields with them and everything. I could tell I was just making them feel uncomfortable. They would hardly talk to me." She relayed how her supervising pastor had called her and told her that she needed to dress up, that the people are used to their pastor wearing a suit and tie. He told her, "You don't need to wear a suit and tie, of course, but you'll get more respect if you, um, dress appropriately." That was a direct quote, she said.

My initial instincts told me this is obviously a case where a male paradigm of what is appropriate is operable. My first inclination was to advise Fran to wear what she darn well wanted and to heck with her supervisor and all those redneck farmers. But something else in me took over. I could sort of see the people there not knowing what to make of a young cowgirl pastor. It would be a crying shame if they did not give her a chance. So I told Fran to meet me at such-and-such mall on Friday. I helped her pick out two or three brightly colored pantsuits that she felt comfortable wearing. She was thrilled. She later told me that it seemed to help. While she would rather be wearing jeans, she could tell how the people appreciated her being dressed differently from them. She told me she was eventually able to wear her jeans around them some without undermining her role as pastor.

Now I am not suggesting that a few good pantsuits will change the world. The moral of the story is Wear Red Underwear. Do whatever you need to do to fulfill the ministry to which you are called, wherever you are sent, without compromising who you are.

While I focus on clothes and image, I recognize this is not the only thing that defines us. People should not be judged by the clothes they wear or the way they look, but the fact is they often are. We exist in a culture where people pay $350.00 for a pair of tennis shoes. Consider the movie *Erin Brockovich*. Erin is a struggling single parent, fond of miniskirts and push-up bras. When she finally lands a secretarial position at a law firm, she ought to be grateful enough to rethink her wardrobe, according to her boss. He told her that she was not very professional and that she was making the other women in the office uncomfortable. With audacity, Erin used her own form of back talk (this is cleaned up a bit): "As long as I am a woman, I am going to dress like a woman, and I don't have to hide it." And then she ends the conversation with, "You might want to rethink those ties." Erin becomes a heroine of the people her firm represents in a landmark case against big industry. She also gains respect without changing her style. On the other hand, Fran stands for being yourself with some modifications out of respect for the people with whom you work. Both approaches are right! Those who are looking for one right answer in every situation will not be comforted by this. I hope that the church will increasingly accept multiple styles and allow its leaders to be themselves and to use their gifts in ministry. Wearing red underwear is metaphorically a way of talking back to narrow-minded understandings of what a minister should look like or how he or she should be. It is a way of opening up those understandings, a way of change.

How a Korean Woman Pastor Broke Cultural Barriers

Rev. Kyunglim Shin Lee recalled a time not very long ago in Korea when Presbyterians did not ordain women and Methodists only would ordain unmarried women. To be ordained, a candidate had to serve three years as the sole pastor of a church, and there was a rule that a married woman could not serve as the only pastor of a church. How convenient! That rule was changed, according to Kyunglim, around 1989. She came to the U.S. with her husband in 1984. When she expressed a desire to go to Garrett-Evangelical Theological Seminary and be ordained, some Korean male clergy attacked her, even harassed her, saying "You don't care. You are ruining our wives. You are selfish. You are supposed to help your husband. Seeking your own career is absurd." Kyunglim ignored this and became the first Korean woman in the M.Div. program at Garrett and one of the first Korean women ordained in the United Methodist Church. Once on a return trip to Korea she reported her occupation on the immigration form as "pastor". She was reprimanded by the immigration officer, "This means *your* occupation. Not your husband's!"

At Korean clergy gatherings it was customary for the wives to meet separately from the pastors. Kyunglim attended such a gathering after being ordained and was told to go with the wives. She talked back, "I'm a pastor, and I'm staying."

At first parishioners in her husband's church refused to address her as Reverend. They objected to the fact that she traveled out of town on her job and vocalized their objection both to her face and behind her back. In Korean culture, pastors' wives are like first ladies. Eventually, according to Kyunglim, the resistance gave way. "I shared my vision and my passion for my ministry with them. I asked them to pray for me and my safe journey in my travels and so that I can make important contributions to the churches, including their church."

Many churches in Asia operate according to a "power over" hierarchical model. The initial success of these churches is waning and new models must emerge, and according to Kwok Pui-lan, women are heralding these new models. She writes:

A church that respects the discipleship of women and partnership of equals has to rethink its patterns of leadership, the meaning of ministry, the mobilization of the laity and the relationship of the church and the community. The exercise of power must be dynamic, fluid, open and transparent.[32]

"Things are changing," she reports. Also, Korean people are now more aware that women are clergy, and it is less of a shock. Kyunglim told me that to cope with the resistance, some Korean clergywomen felt they had to act like men, even to the point of lowering their voice to sound like men. Korean women in the West adopted Western culture. "Now we seem to have gotten past that and can be who we are." Progress has been made for Korean women leaders, but there are still barriers, evident in the fact that Korean women pastors mostly serve caucasian churches because Korean congregations still resist women in an authoritative role. Rev. Sun Hae Hwang also identified this barrier that needs to be broken. Not many Korean American women have successfully served Korean American congregations in the United States. Sun Hae thinks it is because women were sent to Korean American churches that were not healthy in the first place. Any male pastor would have had a difficult time. But because a female was sent, the denominational leadership assumes that female pastors don't work for Korean congregations. Also, because of cultural issues, traditional Korean Americans may not be able to accept females in the pastoral position. They may not be able to see a woman in a role of authority and respect. She calls for church leadership to be more intentional to appoint Korean clergywomen to Korean American churches and to recognize and utilize their individual gifts for Korean American communities.

The Rev. Yong Ja Kim, pastor of Rainbow United Methodist Church in Portland, Maine, is the first Korean American woman to serve a predominantly Korean congregation in her conference. After being refused ordination in Korea, Kim came to New England to pursue her call to ministry. She sees this move as "crossing a Red Sea."[33]

Another Korean woman leader I spoke with objected to my notion of back talk as a strategy for change, saying it would not work in the Korean Church. She feared it would be offensive and immediately shut down communication. I believe she has a point. Culture matters. Yet another Korean clergywoman in Korea told me, "You Americans do not have a monopoly on back talk. We do it all the time in our own way." In Kyunglim's storytelling, I could detect a certain amount of back talk. I think she adapted it and used it in a way that related to her culture. "Koreans are a passionate people," she said, "and they recognize and respect passion and sincerity in others."

Kyunglim is now a highly regarded and respected leader in the Korean Church and in her denomination. In 2003 she was invited with a group of clergy to North Korea for a summit with political leaders. "People express their pride in me. It took me thirteen years, but I won them over."

Strategy #11: Re-train and Educate. Share Your Passion. Never Miss a Teachable Moment.

Many of the women I talked with used this multi-layered strategy. "Talk with people. Win them over," said Rita Callis. "Sit on the porch with them." It is about connecting with people. Rita and Kyunglim both said they respectfully "re-trained" through their preaching and through other actions a little at a time. Kyunglim asked for their prayers. Rita never missed an opportunity to help parishioners see her as human, as one of them. Being a farm girl from the rural south, she was used to the curmudgeonly stubbornness of her parishioners. Drawing on her reservoir of humor and faith, she summoned her authority and challenged them. They listened.

One woman leader in her Quaker community says, "Most people are teachable." The word teachable, related to the Greek word *praos,* is often translated in the New Testament as meek. A much more accurate rendering is the nautical term *yare,* which is when a ship "minds its rudder well." A ship tacking zigzags through the water. Yare is the ability of a ship to straighten itself, to change and adapt. To be unteachable is to rigidly adhere to an external force that will ultimately capsize the ship. Most of us have come up against such resistance. Many of the leaders I interviewed believe that resistance is lessening in the emerging church.

To teach is often to build upon what one already knows or thinks, a pedagogical strategy educators use before the zinger, the idea that will knock one off her or his moorings and create discomfort and dissonance. Most of us know a teacher or someone in our lives who has done this. I thank God my teachers did this. It can help us move to a new place. In her sermons, Rita builds on common ground and judiciously weaves in the hard stuff.

Several women told me about incidents in which their passion for their beliefs became evident through their emotions. "I have always tried to hide my emotions because of the stereotype that women are too emotional," said one. Some believe the absolute worst thing you can do is cry. Crying means (predominantly in Western culture) that you are not in control, that you have broken down, and consequently that you have been broken. The famous line Tom Hanks uttered in the film *A League of Their Own,* "There's no crying in baseball!" has applied to professional ministry.

Jeanne Porter remembered the first time a woman cried in a meeting she attended. She confronted the woman in the restroom with "Don't do that!"

Jeanne thought the woman's tears were fake, for the purpose of manipulating men. At that time she believed that crying, showing emotion, undermined women's authority.[34] One young woman shared with me how a male boss of hers delighted in making women cry on the job. "It was some kind of game with him. I made up my mind not to play." Marjorie Baker believes that it is permissible and even healthy to show emotion. "We have to let them know what we care about. We teach with our passion," she says. We may be more accepting now of tears from both men and women as genuine emotion, but emotion doesn't have to mean tears. Not showing emotion can be acquiescing to male models of leadership. Many leaders recalled significant learning and change coming out of occasions when emotions were freely expressed.

A Female Canon? No Way! Yes, Way!

I had a fascinating conversation with the Rev. Lucy Winkett at St. Paul's Cathedral on January 15, 2004. Lucy Winkett grew up in the Church of England and never seriously rebelled from it. She loved music, felt that was her gift, and was trained in it. She achieved some success as a musician. One day in church she heard a sermon titled "The Appearance of Success." She recognized herself in this sermon as she had all the potential for the trappings of success but felt unfulfilled. She knew instantly, she told me, "that I was going to be ordained." She went to an ecumenical theological college in Birmingham and focused on urban ministry. She was given two field education assignments, first in a mosque where she had "interesting" conversations with the imam. The second was at a black pentecostal congregation. Both experiences were pivotal, and she learned much that would serve her well. She learned from her experience of being around and trying to work with someone who did not recognize her ministry. She was humbled to be "an eavesdropper" in the presence of those whose defining faith experience was resistance to racism and the quest for justice.

Lucy was ordained and sent to East London to serve in a large, economically deprived, diverse parish. She came to St. Paul's for a position as a minor canon, a junior post in cathedral parlance, the first woman priest ever for St. Paul's. Immediately she encountered a wave of resistance. Two priests on the cathedral staff vehemently opposed the ordination of women. When she was appointed there in 1997, the press went crazy, and she found her picture on the front page of the newspapers, a figure of controversy. One of the opposing priests gave a press interview declaring that the church was now broken and the eucharist impaired because of her. The dean of the cathedral supported Lucy, and at a another press conference, in an attempt to quell the controversy, said that she was the right person for the job, and gender had nothing to do with it. A British Broadcasting Corporation (BBC) documentary team followed her around for eighteen months to tell the story of the first woman canon at St. Paul's. When the filmed aired in 1998, she received death threats, but she also received over two thousand letters of support. "I was overwhelmed at this experience of inexplicable grace," she recalled.

The most acute resistance came when she celebrated the eucharist. The two priests who opposed her refused to serve with her. But the issue that broke the camel's back was over the reserved sacrament. In the Anglican tradition, she explained, when the bread and wine are consecrated for use in the eucharist, any unused, leftover portions are kept in reserve in a special vault and brought out to be used in another service. The two priests who opposed her claimed that any elements she consecrated were not the Body of Christ, and they did not want elements she had touched to get mixed up with the Body of Christ consecrated by the male priests. "Essentially they were saying I polluted the sacrament," said Lucy. I told Lucy that I thought this was absurd, much like children pouting. "Well, for them it was a deeply spiritual issue, but this was where I drew the line. Either I am a priest or I am not. That was the line I stood firm on."

The dean of the cathedral backed her, and she stayed. One of the opposing priests left, but the other stayed as well and served with her. It easily could have gone the other way, and Lucy is well aware of this. She was prepared to walk away, having faith that God would send her somewhere. Last year she moved into a new role as residentiary canon, a senior post in the church. At thirty-six years old, she is one of the youngest ever. Now two more female minor canons are on staff at St. Paul's. "The world is about to change here," she prophesies. "I was glad to be able to lance the boil and draw some of the poison out. Now it will be easier for women. Not easy, but easier."

What struck me most about Lucy was her indomitable spirit. Throughout the ordeal with the opposing priests, Lucy maintained relationships with them. "I was unfailingly friendly. I would not allow that nastiness to make me nasty. I was determined to forge a relationship even on an anvil of profound disagreement." And they responded, so good working relationships were made possible. One of the men has since changed his mind and, while not actually apologizing, said he regretted the way they treated her.

Lucy Winkett loves her ministry, from providing pastoral care to home-less people to organizing the queen's Golden Jubilee service. Lucy wrote: "It is the irresistible invitation, the unrefusable, compelling nature of being a priest that holds me and enthralls me. Being a priest for me is about turn-ing my face toward the light."[35] She recalls doing a wedding and a funeral on the same day. "Two families: one distraught, one overjoyed. I must be both." She will serve a seven-year term at the cathedral and then hopes to go to a small parish somewhere, a position that some would view as a step down. She does not view it that way, however; she just sees it as another way to answer God's call. She sees a long road ahead for women in the Anglican Church. "Enslaved peoples have always needed to bond together and sing songs of freedom. The way the church functions leads women to work in isolation from each other. We don't have a critical mass yet," she volunteered. Another hurdle is getting women in the episcopacy in the Anglican Church. When one is in the presence of Lucy Winkett, there is no doubt that she is one whom God has chosen.

Strategy #12: Ignore and Rise Above the Garbage

Ignoring the garbage is not to abandon back talk. It is just knowing when to use it. Back talk should not be wasted on garbage. Lucy Winkett refused to sink to the level of those who opposed her. She maintained her integri-ty and never succumbed to the urge to respond to the nastiness. Sometimes it was very difficult for her to maintain, she admits. She also ignored the taunts of some worshipers, such as, "Why are you trying to become a man?" or "What the hell is she doing in my church?" That this took place so recently (1998–2000) should not shock us. Some women and men are under the illusion that this kind of thing does not happen anymore. British Methodist clergywoman Margaret Jones was told by the male pastor she followed in one parish that an older woman had confided to him that she wanted to die before he left so as not to risk having a woman do her funer-al. Kyunglim Shin Lee did not give in to the attempts to make her feel guilty for not being the traditional pastor's wife. Elsa Florez endured the inappropriate questioning of her ordaining board. Marjorie Baker did not respond in kind when a male committee chair smirked at her.

Ignoring the garbage is sometimes a good idea for at least two reasons: (1) To respond can ignite the flames and make it worse; and (2) Garbage often disappears on its own; some of it is biodegradable. This does not mean that it is not important to fight for what you believe and to defend yourself. It is about saving your energy for what really matters. Up to a point (see the next strategy) Lucy Winkett ignored the pettiness of the opposing priests. Paradoxical to the above strategy of letting our emotions show, Janice Jenkins advises us not to give validity to something by acknowledging that it hurt you. We need to be honest, and not in denial, but to move through it. In the birthing process, this is called pushing through the pain. "This too shall pass" are wise words.

One of the tactics that oppressors use is to ignore those whom they oppress, to attempt to discount or diminish their identity by refusing to hear their voices. This strategy is to turn the tables on that maneuver for better purposes. "Garbage-inflictors" may never go away entirely, but women are rising above them to serve God.

How Eleven Women Caused an Earthquake

I'm often surprised at how many women entering seminary these days have never heard the story of the famous Philadelphia Eleven. It is an amazing story, foundational for women in the church. My sources for this story are Pamela W. Darling, author of *New Wine: The Story of Women Transforming Leadership and Power in the Episcopal Church,* and Mary S. Donovan, author of *A Different Call* and director of the Women's History Project, whom I spoke with by phone. I am summarizing here and hope I can do it justice. The story of how women came to be ordained in the Episcopal Church is a long, involved one described well by Pamela Darling. It did not happen overnight or even in a decade. It was a hard fight. One barrier was broken with the acceptance of women deacons, but it was possible, according to Pamela Darling, for some to accept women deacons without disturbing age-old concepts of women's "proper place." Actually, as she points out, the first woman priest in the Anglican Communion was not an American. In 1944 the bishop of Hong Kong ordained Florence Li Tim-Oi to minister to and serve as priest to Chinese Anglicans under the Japanese Occupation. When word of her ordination reached England, this bishop was reprimanded, and Li Tim-Oi agreed to curtail her priestly functions to avoid punitive action against him. For a long time she was forgotten by many.

There was a lot of talk about women's ordination in the '60s and '70s in the Episcopal Church. "Talk precedes action, especially for Episcopalians," writes Darling.[36] In 1958, the Episcopal Theological School in Cambridge, Massachusetts, became the first Episcopal seminary to admit women, but the church would not ordain them. The talk of women's ordination led to the organization of opposition to it, which gained a lot of steam and threatened schism. Supporters of women's ordination also mobilized. Suzanne (Sue) Hiatt, an ordained deacon and a community organizer, began to build up the network of support.[37] She and another woman organized a conference on women's ministries at Virginia Theological Seminary in 1971. The House of Bishops kept avoiding the idea of ordaining women as priests by appointing study committee after study committee (a well-known strategy of resistance to change). Sue and other supporters of women priests wrote to the presiding bishop that they would boycott any further study committees. They formed the Episcopal Women's Caucus, an organization of seminarians, women deacons, lay leaders, and male supporters. They dedicated themselves to opening the priesthood and episcopate to women. In the fall of 1972 the House of Bishops received the report of the 1971 study committee, which was comprised of only bishops since no women would serve. They voted to accept a measure that supported "in principle" the ordination of women. Many thought that women would be ordained the next year, but the opposition roared. In 1973 a conservative successor was named presiding bishop. A vote to ordain women priests failed because of a technicality in the voting. It was a "stunning defeat," Darling recalls, and brought the first phase of the campaign, where everybody played by the rules of conventional church politics, to an end.[38]

Soon after, Sue Hiatt, Carol Anderson, Carter Heyward, and others began a new tactic to proceed without the approval of the general convention. The rationale they put forth was that the church laws did not explicitly prohibit the ordination of women. They decided to meet for a strategy session in New York in November 1973 with some bishops to discuss the possibility of ordaining women. Everyone present at the session supported women's ordination, but the advice of the bishops was to be patient, sit tight, and "Let us do it for you girls," according to Darling.[39] The women walked out of the meeting. At a diocesan ordination service in December of that year at the Cathedral of St. John the Divine, several women deacons challenged the bishop to present them for ordination. He refused. Again they walked out in protest, joined by many in the congregation. During this time these women were assaulted verbally and even physically by opponents. Sue Hiatt said, "My vocation was not to continue to ask for permission to be a priest, but to be a priest."[40] And on another occasion she stated: "When I owned my call, I tried in very ladylike and reasonable ways to convince the church. . . . Finally it became necessary to act on the call despite the church's desire to delay."[41] They decided to act and so organized an ordination to priesthood to be held in Philadelphia at the Church of the Advocate. On July 29, 1974, the Feasts of Saints Mary and Martha, eleven women deacons were ordained as priests by three retired (or resigned) bishops and one active bishop.[42] Other women deacons declined to present themselves to be priested because of financial dependence on jobs that certainly would be lost, among other reasons. A large crowd including many members of the press witnessed the historical event. The presiding bishop received word of what was planned and contacted the women before the service asking them to reconsider and to wait until canonical changes could be made. The women were through waiting.

The Philadelphia ordinations caused an earthquake in the church and were ruled irregular, but the women laid claim to a higher authority of the "conscience informed by the Holy Spirit." They felt the church was opposing God's will in regard to women. Authorities were furious. Some supporters of women's ordination felt this act of defiance would hurt the cause. On August 14, 1974, the House of Bishops called an emergency session and declared the ordinations invalid, refusing to speak directly with the women. The women knew at the outset their ordinations would be challenged. Though the House of Bishops never formally retracted their statement (that the ordinations were invalid), most came to accept them. No disciplinary action was taken against the women, but charges were filed against the ordaining bishops. Meantime, the new priests conducted public services, and a second irregular ordination was planned. Many felt that women were now priests in the Episcopal Church, and there was nothing that could be done to stop it. Others felt the legal situation had to be resolved. A change in a canon law that allowed for women's ordination to the priesthood was presented to the general convention in 1976. The House of Bishops voted to accept it. The next day the House of Delegates (laity) did as well. Participants recalled weeping and embracing. The story is far from over, according to Pamela Darling and Mary Donovan. The transformation of the Episcopal Church will continue. Some declare the Philadelphia Eleven to be saints while others still deny their ordination though they were "regularized" in 1977. The courage and fortitude of these women serves as a model. Sometimes you have to just do it.

Strategy #13: Draw the Line

Lucy Winkett drew the line when the priests more or less called the elements she consecrated "tainted." For her the place to draw the line was the spiritual efficacy of the sacraments. She said, "This is the line I would not cross." This is risky business, and sometimes we take the fall and have the battle scars to prove it.

Sometimes you have to be prepared to walk away. We don't want to make idle threats but choose our battles. We don't often draw the line in the sand and dare someone to cross it. At some point things are beyond compromise. You have to take a stand and be prepared to defend it. This is the flipside of Strategy #3. There are some things you cannot ignore, some things you have to say "no" to. Marjorie Procter-Smith speaks about the "power of the fast" of saying no, the power of refusal and negation.[43] A symbolic act of negation was a theological necessity for Lucy Winkett.

The Philadelphia Eleven knew where they drew the line. They knew they would no longer wait around for the Episcopal Church to ordain them. They would stop asking permission. It was a matter of conscience. Advocates for change use both institutional tactics (lobbying, petitions, letter writing) and extra-institutional tactics such as the "irregular" ordinations and "illegitimate" celebrations of the eucharist. Sociologists observe that advocates for change usually begin with the former, but move to extra-institutional tactics as the social movement gains steam. Organizational elites who have a stake in current organizational structure or who have the most to lose are slower to move to extra-institutional tactics.[44] Drawing the line may serve to force the hand of someone or some organization that is dragging its feet, breaking a pattern of accommodating to others' demands. Again, one has to be prepared to take the consequences. In the summer of

2002, seven Catholic women were ordained by a renegade Roman Catholic bishop in Austria. The women were immediately excommunicated. In the past the church has stressed that excommunication is to be imposed only for the most serious offenses. The Code of Canon Law details only nine offenses that call for excommunication, and a woman receiving ordination is not one of them.[45] In this case one might presume that the extra-institutional, draw-the-line strategy backfired. These women implemented a courageous witness, and though the results were not what were hoped for, I believe their actions serve a greater purpose. Sometimes you come up against the limits of talk, when talking doesn't help anymore. Then action itself becomes back talk.

A Woman to Reckon With

I'll never forget the day I met Shirley Randall. Shirley is a feisty, staunchly devout laywoman who wears about fifteen hats at the Louis W. Foxwell Memorial Apartments (she described it as Section 8 housing for the handicapped, disabled, and elderly). She greeted me with a huge, warm smile. Though Shirley is a woman of constant motion, I got her to sit down with me to tell her story. She was born to deaf parents in a poor family. They were grounded in the church, and her faith has seen her through life. She was the mouthpiece for her mother, talking and listening for her, learning sign language very early. "Everything that came out of my mouth was not about me, but to speak for the deaf." Consequently she became very precocious and sassy, she told me. She had to talk back because she is black, a woman, and a child of the deaf community.

Shirley laughingly recalled being taught cuss words at age nine or ten so she could cuss out the bill collectors for her mother. She would go to the doctor with her mother and have to explain complex medical procedures to advocate for her. She remembered an incident on a bus. She was sitting with her mother and signing to her. Someone across the aisle said, "Oh, they must be deaf and dumb." Shirley stood up and said, "You must be hearing and dumb! I can hear what you're saying. My mama is not dumb!" Her mother died in 1987, but she was the one who led Shirley to her current ministry (and she does consider it her ministry).

Louis Foxwell was the pastor of a deaf church they attended. After he died the apartments were built in his memory. "My mother told me she believed God meant me for this role." Shirley continues to advocate for the deaf and for other residents every day. For example, cab drivers would refuse to take people in wheelchairs. She quickly straightened them out. Police would not respond to complaints there because they believed "all those people should be institutionalized." Shirley met with law enforcement officials, began doing training workshops to sensitize the police to the needs of the residents, and has briefed officers on their morning roll call. "I have been called 'a villager' because I try to bring peace to any situation."

She describes herself as boisterous. "I was kicked out of a church once," she said. She was active in a large African American congregation, helping to start their deaf ministry. She felt, though, that the pastor was more interested in "looking good" (looking like they were helping the deaf) rather than really ministering. She raised the issue of paying the interpreters required for every service and church event but was told, "Jesus did not get paid. You all should do it for free." She proposed they hold a deaf sensitivity day to help integrate the deaf ministry into the life of the congregation. For two years she made this proposal and hounded the pastor, only to be ignored. She finally raised a little hell about it, criticizing the pastor in public for his lack of interest. A few days later she received a letter saying there will be no more deaf ministry. "I moved on to other things," she said. "People have great respect for church leaders in the black community and they should not betray that," she admonished.

Shirley is one who lives every moment to the fullest, seeing what she can do for someone else, throwing parties, grandmothering, celebrating birthdays, helping to negotiate insurance forms and bank statements. She is definitely a force to be reckoned with, living out her call to talk back for change!

Strategy #14: Be Firm, Be Faithful

I asked Shirley Randall what some of her strategies for change were. She said immediately, "Be firm, be faithful." She talked about knowing the right thing to do and then having the guts to do it. Be firm. She insisted that the police change their attitude, and she is working to make that happen. She would not let the church off the hook with a "feel good" approach to deaf ministry. Even though she was not able to make definitive progress in that congregation, she was a voice for change. "I made myself heard." Now she's working on another church. "I came along in the time where women did all the work with none of the recognition. I worked myself onto some committees, in decision-making roles." Shirley told me that although she knows the church is sexist and the last to get it right, she still receives a great deal of spiritual nourishment and empowerment. from it. Though she is somewhat disillusioned right now, I could see Shirley's spiritual depth, that she is undergirded by prayer and driven by her faith in God. "Be faithful," she advised. Miriam Therese Winter captures Shirley well when she says that "at the heart of feminist women's spirituality is telling it like it is."[46] Shirley's mother was her inspiration. She shared with me about women in the deaf community, a sisterhood, who taught her "not to be ashamed of who I am." She remembered eight of them gathering in a bathroom to check out her menstrual problems! She could never move very far away from their center. "These women taught me to stick up for what I know is right and always end with a smile." Back talk is thought of as disrespect for one's elders. For Shirley, it was just the opposite. Her back talk came from tapping into the wisdom of these women.

Margaret Mead once said, "The most creative force in the world is the menopausal woman with zest." This strategy and variations on it was a theme that was consistent with many of the women's stories. It is about not compromising on the issues of greatest importance. It is about remaining steadfast. It is about delivering the message over and over, firmly, without hedging, without backing down, never-letting-them-see-you-sweat, not blinking first. One woman advised, "Use your fear." Fear is not the absence of courage; it creates courage. Receive strength from sources of wisdom that came before you. Being firm and faithful, women and men are bringing change in the church and in the world.

▪ 5 ▪

TOO MUCH TALK
The Limits of Talk in Creating Change

LANGUAGE IS A TREMENDOUS GIFT, and we continue to strive to be stewards of it and to use it wisely. Writers and poets and preachers know that words are hugely powerful with the ability to move us, to anger us, to teach us, to shock or seduce us, to change us. Of course, words are not the only things that can do this, and words can often be empty and cruel and get in the way. One of the limits of talk is that it fails many times to be the best way to communicate.

There are other forms of communication, such as body language, dance, sexual expression, sign language, music, and all kinds of art forms. Mostly these ways are more effective than words, or at least communicate in ways that words cannot. There is an often-quoted axiom, "Preach the Gospel at all times. If necessary, use words." Sometimes there are just no words to express the momentous, the beautiful, the tragic. Yes, words are powerful, but they have their limits. The psalmist describes it this way:

> The heavens are telling the glory of God;
> and the firmament proclaims God's handiwork.
> Day to day pours forth speech, and night to night
> declares knowledge.
> There is no speech, nor are there words;
> their voice is not heard;
> yet their voice goes out through all the earth,
> their words to the end of the world.
>
> (Psalms 19:1–4)

Rebecca Chopp describes how this limit of talk particularly affects women. She says that language, as we know it, has been unable or inadequate or perhaps unwilling to give voice to women's experience.[1] We know that words fail to describe God; we cannot capture what the heavens are telling. Yet the church has insisted that when trying to talk about this mystery, that we rely solely upon male-conceived reality. At times women were denied access to language, compelled to silence. In some cultures women are veiled and silenced, not to be seen or heard. Veiling women was widespread, one historian suggests, because women were regarded as male property, and men did not want other men to see and/or take their property.[2]

Girls and women have been denied education and literacy. Even so, they find ways to communicate and talk back. No perfect feminist speech exists, according to Deborah Cameron, but we are moving toward a radical discourse of emancipation so that language does not control us.[3] One inspiring example is Harriet Powers. Born a slave in Georgia in 1837, she was able to articulate through her fingers and her soul in her amazing quilts that told stories of freedom. *Hidden in Plain View: A Secret Story of Quilts and the Underground Railroad* by Raymond Dobard and Jacqueline Tobin tells how quilts, which could be laid out to air without arousing suspicion, gave slaves directions for their escape. Quilt images like the log cabin, the wagon wheel, and shoofly signaled slaves how to prepare for their journey. Stitching patterns created maps that showed slaves the best routes to flee. Sometimes survival under conditions of oppression required what Katie Cannon calls "skills of acquiescence," of "invisible dignity, quiet grace and unshouted courage."[4] It is not false consent but recognition of the limitation of language. A long-standing tradition of protest art, such as Picasso's *Guernica* and street art, attests to the need to talk back without words. Kelly Brown Douglas identified a "sexual discourse of resistance" that exposes the stereotypes imposed by white culture and helps to foster more life-enhancing views for oppressed peoples.[5]

Deborah Cameron confirmed that linguistic data on all sorts of "muted groups" (silenced groups of people) indicates that they do generate specific ways of speaking, but they will engage in what is called "code switching" in order to communicate with the dominant group and function in society. It may be akin to the double consciousness experienced by African Americans. A term coined by W. E. B. DuBois in *The Souls of Black Folks* in 1903, double consciousness refers to only being allowed to be viewed through the eyes of others, of having to live in two worlds, where someone else names reality for you. Yet as Cameron conveys, muted groups are ceasing to allow dominant groups to name reality and control their language.[6] I found this to be true of the Deaf Culture. Though American Sign Language (ASL) is a way of "talking," it is done without speaking verbally. Rev. Peggy Johnson helped me to understand that ASL is the first language of people of the Deaf Culture. It is different from English. English is the second language or even the third of many of the American Sign Language users in this country. A sign language does not have the same grammar and syntax of English. Yet we have a bias that everybody here ought to speak and know English. Even written documents, texts, instructions, etc., often do not translate well into American Sign Language. We do not all speak the same languages and may not understand each other. The diversity of language is on the one hand a limitation of talk, but on the other, a potential plus. More languages, more ways to talk back!

There is no word for sass or back talk in ASL. Yet deaf people do back talk, according to interpreter Carol Stevens. People in Deaf Culture are good at being blunt. "Gray fuzzy niceties" do not exist in ASL, says Peggy Johnson. They back talk to each other and sometimes to those who patronize them. Their talking back to systems of oppression or being heard may depend on the accessibility of an interpreter. If there is no interpreter, people who use ASL often have either to acquiesce or show their anger or frustration physically. Elke Betz-Schmidt said, "I have had to talk back my whole life." She says:

> People tend to impose pre-conceived limits on deaf people. I was placed in remedial classes because I was deaf. I wasn't slow. I just needed support and understanding of my potential. Today, I have similar obstacles in conveying my passion and unique gifts for the complexity of Deaf Ministry to my conference. My challenge and desire is to help them comprehend and embrace the role I feel called to fill in the church.[7]

Al Couthen reminded me of the time some years ago when members of Deaf Culture demanded a deaf president of Galludet University. The person originally chosen for the job knew very little about Deaf Culture and did not know sign language. A book, *The Week The World Heard Galludet* by Jack Gannon, tells that story. Al is an active back talker himself as president

of the National Black Deaf Advocates, which he was instrumental in start-
ing because the National Association for the Deaf is mostly a white organization. They are working to get more job opportunities for the deaf, more
accessibility to health services, more closed caption in the media.

Another limit of talk that I have alluded to is the dangerous nature of
"talking back." We live in cultures today that are hostile to women's well-
being. Every year 683,000 women are raped, according to the National
Victim Center. That number is low because it only includes reported rapes.
Each year approximately two million women are physically or sexually
assaulted or stalked by an intimate partner in the U.S.[8] I was shocked to
learn that 3 percent of the women in the U.S. military experienced sexual
assault in one year (2,002 reported cases). One hundred twenty-nine female
soldiers in the Middle East have reported sexual assault. Their injuries were
officially reported as the result of "friendly fire" by the military. According
to Joanna Starek, "When women push their way onto male turf, some men
push back."[9] Today the U.S. government estimates that globally 700,000
women and children are victims of human trafficking or modern-day slav-
ery.[10] The Asia Foundation says it is impossible to even guess the number of
women victims of violence across Asia. Inadequate legal structures in much
of Asia effectively condone violence against women.[11] The Circle of African
Women Theologians have decried the deplorable conditions for women
across Africa with rape, genital mutilation, and prostitution commonplace.[12]
Violence against women is pervasive, but it is tempting to bracket this as
only happening to a few. The pervasiveness of violence against women is
symbolic and points to the enduring underlying misogynist assumption
that women are inferior and deserve to be punished if they rebel against
being told they are inferior. Several women I interviewed were survivors of
abuse. They told me that overt back talk is dangerous and would just get
them more abuse. All of these women without exception declared that they
found other ways to talk back through writing, art, music, and learning;
ultimately, this was what gave them the courage to walk out.

Historically, a lot of silence was imposed on and required of women in
the church. Biblical writings meant for certain groups in a particular time
and place were "doctrinized" by the church. Virginia Ramey Mollenkott,
noted professor and author, recalled a teacher in her Presbyterian high
school that said, "When women do theology, the result is always heresy." In
this and other ways, girls were silenced. She also reflected that in one sense

the teacher's remark is true. "If androcentric theology is the norm, then women do introduce heresy."[13] Women were told to shut up, were interrupted, told their words were wrong or silly, even punished, so many gave up.

The story of Sor Juana Inés de la Cruz, a seventeenth-century nun from Mexico, is a case in point. She was known for her brilliance, her beautiful poetry, and theological genius. It seemed she was recognized as a female intellectual in a world where women were oppressed and looked down upon. She was invited to the court of the Marquis, where she wrote and studied under royal protection for a time. When the Marquis's term ended, however, that protection dissolved. Juana's prominence earned her the wrath of some envious enemies. A bishop published her work under a pen name, with his own introduction accusing her of being immature and stupid. She published a response in which she defended her rights as a woman and all women's rights to education. She forthrightly presented her thoughts about gender roles and the equality of women and men. This proclamation effectively ended her career as a public intellectual. Under threat of severe persecution, she was forced to stop writing and to sell her books and musical instruments. Some scholars believe she did this more as an act of penitence than of acquiescence. According to legend, she was forced to sign in her own blood "I, Sor Juana, worst of all." Even though she was threatened and censored, Sor Juana managed for a time to break the silence that women had been forced to keep.[14]

Research on women's talk, as Deborah Cameron indicates, illumines the fact that women have always rebelled against being silenced. They talked anyway. Nor are they inarticulate. More hidden history of women's speech and writing is emerging. Women do have rich verbal and nonverbal resources.[15] The stories that have grown up around many of the saints are of course embellished, but they still arouse and prove illustrative. Saint Christina, called "Christina the Astonishing," lived seventeen centuries ago. According to one Web site, Christina was a sort of "Tomb Raidin', Ass-Kickin' Saint" who might wear leather strides and steel-toe boots if she were still around today. Christina had her tongue cut out, which was a common torture during the persecutions. According to tradition she picked it up and threw it in her torturer's face, and he was blinded immediately. Talk about talking back without talking!

When silence is attempted to be forced, imposed on others to keep them in their place, it becomes a tool of domination. People who have been "shushed" or, figuratively speaking, had their tongues cut out, tend to view silence as bad. Yet silence too is a form of communication. Sharon Ringe wrote about learning the "power of articulation and the art of silence" in her commitment to affirming the full humanity of all women and men. The first of those comes from women reclaiming "language as our own." Finding and knowing the right words to say can take you far. The second comes when the wealthy, powerful people learn to be quiet, to hear the voices of those who are poor and powerless, "who call us to account for the consequences of our lives."[16]

How does one describe the art of silence? Quakers know it well—this waiting for God. In silence Quakers find a deepening process bringing them into their hearts where they meet God. A Quaker is asked to speak only if it will improve upon the silence. As a community soaked in silence, friends seek and experience a greater awareness and responsibility toward one another. In this chattering world, the notion of silence becomes even more needed, more meaningful.[17]

In our "wireless generation," cell phones, instant messaging, and distance learning are everywhere. In contemporary Western culture, we are afraid of silence. All pauses and gaps must be filled. While there are contexts in which silence is negative, as I mentioned above, the spiritual practice of silence can allow us to transcend our chattering world. Talk is cheap. But I still believe in talk.

Unzo Lee, a Korean American Presbyterian clergywoman, confronted the Western emphasis on speech and honors the Asian cultural understandings of silence. Silence, she says, is not the absence of speech, but like a bowl waiting to be filled. In silence a person waits to be filled up before speaking. Silence can be an act of resistance as long as it is chosen and not forced. Silence is, then, a way of talking back. Lee recalls a proverb often quoted to silence women: "A crowing hen will come to no good end." She re-invents the proverb, "When women crow, we had better lay eggs." To lay eggs, she reflects, is to enflesh the words, to incarnate the Word, to walk the talk.[18] We do not lack for talk. Maybe not all of it is idle discourse, but I ask, what is the legacy of language that we leave? Will we know how to talk back when the time comes?

▪ 6 ▪

BACK TALK ON THE FRONTLINE

People are talking. They are talking back in a multitude of ways. Women and men are talking back in the social and cultural arenas, agitating for change, challenging unjust structures, demanding a leveling of the playing field. Still, among the millions who are poor, the majority of them are women and children. Violence against women is still the norm. Women still earn less than men do. Things are worse for Latino, African, Asian, and African American women. The time is at hand for some serious back talk.

Women who enter areas traditionally dominated by men are effectively talking back. Women leaders are creating positive change in the church, redefining it and leading it in new directions. We are talking back to the long-standing traditions of Christianity, to denominational structures and hierarchies, and to individuals who resist our leadership. Back talk is a ministry of conversion. Strategies for change are places where God has gone before us and will continue to lead us. Within these strategies is the Christian call to conversion, to *metanoia* for all of us, incumbent on all of us. It is to live a life bent on conversion that continually turns toward God. To live bent on conversion, in contrast to living "bent on conquest," as Joan Chittister eloquently puts it, is to live "welcoming of the tomorrow that is already in embryo rather than to attempt to cement today into eternity."[1] Back talk calls the church to live bent on conversion.

Women and men are challenging the ways we have understood the church and ministry. They have talked back and continue to talk back to hierarchical ways of being that serve those in power and marginalize everyone else. They are talking back to leadership styles of domination and competition. They are talking back to spiritual emptiness, close-mindedness, and dishonesty. Diana Hayes points out the model of womanist theologians who shatter the complacent image of the black church, exposing its inability to serve as a vehicle of liberation within the black community. She says that in their provocative discourse, womanists challenge the uncritical sexism, the homophobia, and other forms of resistance that have "made their home within the bosom of the black church."[2]

It is my hope that men and women will find reasons to shout, reasons to laugh and cry, and motivations to act from these stories and strategies. Individuals will have to relearn how to talk and how to walk. As I have tried to convey, the strategies are not tricks, techniques, or sure-fire steps, but represent in the aggregate a road map of places to go for strength for the journey. People I interviewed said we can make change happen; it can be done. A sculpture begins with a few chips of the rock. We are sculpting great works out of barriers and walls of stone.

Here again are the strategies in summary:

- **Strategy #1:** Take advantage of tension and "the right time" (pp. 84–86). Timing is important, but we can create a sense of urgency as Dr. Janice Jenkins, Rev. Kenny Smith, and other leaders in the Northern Virginia Baptist Association did. Discern the right time, and go for it.

- **Strategy #2:** Work with the leadership (pp. 86–88). Change can occur from the inside out or from the bottom up. Like women in the Northern Virginia Baptist Association, find allies on the inside to get your foot in the door. Don't dismiss out of hand help from any source.

- **Strategy #3:** Stick it out with Chutzpa (pp. 89–91). Like Elsa Florez, don't give up easily. Stick it out without repressing your pain. Show your chutzpa when everyone thinks you can't hack it. Talk back and let them know you are not going away.

- **Strategy #4:** Create a coalition (pp. 93–94). Gather strength and wisdom from others and enlist an army of workers for change, as Janice Jenkins, Marjorie Baker, and Christina Rees did. Make a workable plan, and don't try to go it alone.

- **Strategy #5:** Do your homework: Engage in theological reflection (pp. 95–96). Know what you are talking about and why change is necessary. Correlate your experience with the biblical and theological heritage of the faith, advises Christina Rees. Don't just complain; justify an alternative vision.

- **Strategy #6:** Have a sense of humor and use it (pp. 98–100). Don't forget to keep your perspective. Be able to laugh at yourself like Rita Callis and to make others laugh to diffuse tough situations, but be aware of the potential trivialization sometimes caused by humor.

- **Strategy #7:** Be clear about your call, about who you are and what gifts you bring (pp. 100–102). Know beyond the shadow of a doubt that God has called you and has given you gifts for ministry. Go confident in grace, as Rita Callis says.

- **Strategy #8:** Lobby for change (pp. 106–107). Gather supporters and then work on other people to change their minds. Make a plan and stick to it. Explain patiently, says Christina Rees, why change is a good idea.

- **Strategy #9:** Mentor and befriend colleagues (pp. 109–11). Bring affirmation to women's leadership by mentoring other women and being mentored. Tell stories of change. Work against amnesia regarding the struggles of women.

- **Strategy #10:** Wear red underwear (pp. 111–113). Do not lose your identity, your "self" in conforming to rules. Challenge accepted notions of ministry and what ministers look like. If you can't change people overnight, make some adaptations in the interim.

- **Strategy #11:** Re-train and educate (pp. 116–117). Share your passion. Never miss a teachable moment. Educate folks into a new understanding of church and leadership. Do not be afraid of sharing your feelings. Break barriers as many Korean clergywomen are doing.

- **Strategy #12:** Ignore and rise above the garbage (pp. 119–120). Do not succumb to the temptation to respond in kind to nastiness.

Canon Lucy Winkett attests to being "unfailingly friendly" in the midst of great tribulation.

- **Strategy #13:** Draw the line (pp. 123–124). Even so, know where you draw the line, says Lucy Winkett. Sometimes you have to move forward out of an impasse. Remember the Philadelphia Eleven. There may come a time when you have to stop asking permission and just be.

- **Strategy #14:** Be firm. Be faithful (pp. 125–126). State your case without flinching, according to Shirley Randall. Do not let people off the hook. Remain faithful to where you come from, to your God.

Using some of these fourteen strategies and more, back talkers are slowly midwifing miracles. They are dismantling patriarchy in the church. They are getting churches that have refused to ordain women for centuries or generations to reverse that long-held stand. They are challenging prevailing understandings of church—who is in and who is out, and constrictions on what is a faith community and how people practice that faith. They are providing hospitality to the stranger, the drunkards, the demonized, and the disillusioned. They are changing the way we understand leadership. Not content with the leaders telling others what to do and how to get things done, they insist upon leadership from the underside, calling for an energized and ignited laity. These back talkers are dispelling old notions of what an ordained pastor looks like and how he or she acts. They are proving the competence of women in all kinds of ministries. They are challenging the male-dominated interpretation of scripture, worship, and preaching—putting a new face on ministry. They are refusing to be run off. They are hanging tough, demanding to be included at the core, refusing to be silenced. They are not compromising the values of the gospel and holding the church accountable to living out its message. They are not letting the church off the hook because it is only human. They are not letting it get away with fraud anymore, demanding spiritual and theological integrity. They are insisting on a "de-fossilization" of the church, on what Miriam Therese Winter calls a "living liturgy" that isn't just a re-enactment of a rite, but a lively, dynamic experience that values what we all bring to it.[3]

Back talkers have hit the ground running and are responding to the needs of the world, enlarging their territory, thinking outside the steeple.

They are expanding hearts and enlisting followers after the gospel, breaking all kinds of gender and cultural barriers. The church is raising up a new crop of people who are called, claimed, and connected, who are filled with the spirit—a new tradition of back talk. We can't put them through the same old cookie press so they lose their distinctive shape and voice.

Today's church back talkers are connected to but not living in the past. They revere and seek wisdom from those saints of the struggle. They are eschatological, living toward the future and calling for the new creation when we really do understand and live out the meaning of the *imago dei,* and where we really live out Galatians 3:28 and dispense with confining either/or categories. We will be proud to say we have some good back talkers among us! The church, with all of its flaws but in all of its grace, is compelled to listen.

I leave you with this blessing by an unknown author from Canada:

> May God bless you with discomfort at easy answers,
> half-truths, superficial relationships, so that you will
> live deep within your heart.
> May God bless you with anger at injustice, oppression
> and exploitation of people, so that you will work for
> justice, equity and peace.
> May God bless you with tears to shed for those who suffer
> from pain, rejection, starvation and war, so that you will
> reach out your hand to comfort them and change their pain
> to joy.
> May God bless you with the foolishness to think that you can
> make a difference in the world, so that you will do the
> things which others tell you cannot be done.[4]

And may you always find some boisterous back talk to be blazing in your heart and boldly on your lips!

NOTES

Chapter 1. Back Talk!

1. Janet L. Weathers, "Gender and Small Group Communication in the Church," in *Women, Gender, and Christian Community,* eds. Jane Dempsey Douglass and James F. Kay (Louisville: Westminster John Knox Press, 1997), 117.

2. bell hooks, *Talking Back: Thinking Feminist, Thinking Black* (Boston: South End Press, 1989), 5.

3. Danielle Crittenden, "Let's Junk the Feminist Slogans: The War's Over," *Chatelaine* (August 1990), 38.

4. Ellen Goodman, "Unfriendly Fires in the Gender Wars," *The Washington Post,* April 10, 2004.

5. Frances Mascia-Lees and Patricia Sharpe, *Taking a Stand in a Postfeminist World: Toward an Engaged Cultural Criticism* (New York: State University of New York Press, 2000), 3.

6. Susan Faludi, *Backlash: The Undeclared War Against American Women* (New York: Anchor Books, 1991).

7. Carter Heyward, *Staying Power: Reflections on Gender, Justice and Compassion* (Cleveland: The Pilgrim Press, 1995), x.

8. Rebecca S. Chopp, *The Power to Speak: Feminism, Language, God* (New York: Crossroad Publishing Co., 1989), 22.

9. Barbara Kellerman, "You've Come a Long Way Baby—And You've Got Miles to Go," in *The Difference Difference Makes: Women and Leadership,* ed. Deborah L. Rhode (Stanford: Stanford University Press, 2003), 53.

10. Heyward, *Staying Power,* 53–54.

11. Chopp, *Power to Speak,* 2.

12. Marjorie Procter-Smith, *Praying With Our Eyes Open: Engendering Feminist Liturgical Prayer* (Nashville: Abingdon Press, 1995), 30.

13. Rhode, ed., *Difference,* 19–20.

14. John R. Matthews, S.T.M., *Are Women Clergy Changing the Nature and Practice of Ministry?* (Columbus, Ohio: The Midwest Ministry Development Service, 1996), 2.

15. Mary C. Grey, *Beyond the Dark Night: A Way Forward for the Church?* (London: Cassell, 1997), 116.

16. Patricia Farris and Barbara Troxell, "One Eye on the Past, One Eye on the Future: Women's Contributions to Renewal of the United Methodist Church," *Quarterly Review* (Spring 1998): 37.

17. George Barna Research Group, www.religioustolerance.org.

18. Robert Bezille, ed., *Religion in America* (Princeton: Princeton Religion Research Center, 1993), 43.

19. Princeton Religion Research Center, *Emerging Trends* 23, no. 1 (January 2001).

20. James F. Kay, "Becoming Visible: Baptism, Women, and the Church," in Douglass and Kay, *Women, Gender, and Christian Community*, 92.

21. Mark Chaves, *Ordaining Women: Culture and Conflict in Religious Organizations* (Cambridge: Harvard University Press, 1997), 5.

22. Diana L. Hayes, *Hagar's Daughters: Womanist Ways of Being in the World* (New York: Paulist Press, 1995), 27.

23. Delores C. Carpenter, *A Time For Honor: A Portrait of African American Clergywomen* (St. Louis: Chalice Press, 2001), 20.

24. Kwok Pui-lan, *Introducing Asian Feminist Theology* (Cleveland: The Pilgrim Press, 2000), 98.

25. Barna Research Group, www.religioustolerance.org. Other statistics give even less percentage of women senior pastors.

26. Susan E. Nagle, "Continuity and Change: Women as Pastors," *Lutheran Partners* 11, no. 4 (July–August 1995): 14–15.

27. Matthews, *Women Clergy*, 1.

28. Gracia Fay Ellwood, "Should Men Be Ordained? A Theological Challenge," in *The Wisdom of Daughters: Two Decades of the Voice of Christian Feminism,* ed. Reta Halteman Finger and Kari Sandhaas (Philadelphia: Innisfree Press, 2001), 73.

29. Quoted in *Defecting in Place: Women Claiming Responsibility for Their Own Spiritual Lives* by Miriam Therese Winter, Adair Lummis, and Allison Stokes (New York: Crossroad Press, 1995), 21.

30. "Women Are the Backbone of the Christian Congregations in America," www.Webminister.com, 06, 14, 2001.

31. Ibid.

32. Rhode, *Difference,* 3, 6–7. For example, in government, even though women constitute over half of American voters, only 25 percent of senior executive branch officials, 22 percent of state legislators, 16 percent of mayors of large cities, and 6 percent of state governors are women. The U.S. ranks fiftieth in the percentage of women elected to legislative office. www.womensnews.org.

33. Rhode, *Difference,* 7.

34. Sheron C. Patterson, *New Faith: A Black Christian Woman's Guide to Reformation, Re-Creation, Rediscovery, Renaissance, Resurrection, and Revival* (Minneapolis: Fortress Press, 2000), 18–19.

35. Carolyn Heilbrun, *Writing a Woman's Life* (New York: Ballantine Books, 1988), 18.

36. Barbara Kellerman, "You've Come a Long Way Baby," 58.

37. Phyllis Chesler, *Woman's Inhumanity to Woman* (New York: Thunder's Mouth Press, 2002), 336–37.

38. Chopp, *Power to Speak,* 7.

39. Kellerman, "You've Come a Long Way Baby," 55, 58.

40. Pui-lan, *Introducing Asian Feminist Theology,* 107–8.

41. Carpenter, *A Time For Honor,* 32–33.

42. Letty M. Russell, *Church in the Round: Feminist Interpretation of the Church* (Louisville: Westminster/John Knox Press, 1993), 20.

43. Ibid., 26.

44. Procter-Smith, *Praying With Our Eyes Open,* 13.

45. hooks, *Talking Back,* 9.

46. Dennis Jacobson, *Doing Justice: Congregations and Community Organizing* (Minneapolis: Fortress Press, 2001), 65–66.

47. Darrell L. Guder, *The Continuing Conversion of the Church* (Grand Rapids: William B. Eerdmans Press, 2000), 193.

48. Ann Delorey, "Conservative Renewal Movements and the Threat to the Liberative Power of the Christian Tradition for Women in the Presbyterian Church USA" (M.T.S. thesis, Wesley Theological Seminary, May 2001).

49. Rosemary Ruether and Eleanor McLaughlin, eds., *Women of Spirit: Female Leadership in the Jewish and Christian Traditions* (Eugene: Wipf and Stock Publishers, 1998), 19.

50. Guder, *The Continuing Conversion,* 165.

51. Patterson, *New Faith,* 13.

Chapter 2. Holy Conversations, Holy Change

1. Jay Conger, et al., eds., *The Leader's Change Handbook: An Essential Guide to Setting Direction and Taking Action* (San Francisco: Harper and Row, 1999), xxxv.

2. Ibid., 55.

3. Ibid.

4. The Rev. Peggy Johnson, interview, Baltimore, Maryland, April 17, 2004.

5. Chopp, *Power to Speak,* 21.

6. Thomas Groome, *Educating for Life: A Spiritual Vision for Every Teacher and Parent* (Allen, Tex.: Thomas More, 1998), 17.

7. Shirley Nelson, "Prospecting," in *Rattling Those Dry Bones: Women Changing the Church,* ed. June Steffensen Hagen (San Diego: LuraMedia, 1995), 32.

8. Interview, June 16, 2002.

9. Heyward, *Staying Power,* 55.

10. Jürgen Moltmann, *Theology of Hope: On the Ground and the Implications of a Christian Eschatology* (New York: Harper and Row Publishers, 1967), 320.

11. See Procter-Smith, *Praying With Our Eyes Open,* 49; Beverly Wildung Harrison, *Making the Connection: Essays in Feminist Social Ethics* (Boston: Beacon Press, 1985), 14; Judith V. Jordan, ed., *Women's Growth in Diversity* (New York: The Guilford Press, 1997), 199–208.

12. Natalie K. Watson, *Feminist Theology* (Grand Rapids: Eerdmans Publishing Co., 2003), 100.

13. Matthews, *Women Clergy,* 4.

14. Such as the Rolf Memming Longitudinal Clergy Study and the Clergywomen's Retention Study of the Anna Howard Shaw Center, Boston University School of Theology, October 1997.

15. Rosemary Ruether, *Sexism and God-Talk: Toward a Feminist Theology* (Boston: Beacon Press, 1993), 193.

16. Rhode, *Difference,* 6.

17. Deborah Tannen, *Gender and Discourse* (New York: Oxford University Press, 1994), 3.

18. Rhode, *Difference,* 4–5.

19. Tannen, *Gender and Discourse,* 3–4.

20. Matthews, *Women Clergy,* 2.

21. Leslie Milk, "Girls Rule," in *The Washingtonian Magazine* (September 2001), 68–69.

22. Ibid.

23. Ibid.

24. Matthews, *Women Clergy,* 3.

25. Carol E. Becker, *Leading Women: How Church Women Can Avoid Leadership Traps and Negotiate the Gender Maze* (Nashville: Abingdon Press, 1996), 56.

26. Debra E. Meyerson and Robin J. Ely, "Using Difference to Make a Difference" in Rhode, *Difference,* 135.

27. Chopp, *Power to Speak,* 107, 110.

28. Sara Butler, "Embodiment: Women and Men, Complementary," in *The Church Women Want: Catholic Women in Dialogue,* ed. Elizabeth A. Johnson (New York: Crossroad Publishing Co., 2002), 36, 39, 42. See also Anne-Louise Eriksson, *The Meaning of Gender in Theology: Problems and Possibilities* (Uppsala: Acta Universitatis Upsaliensis, 1995). Eriksson concludes that in spite of Elisabeth Schüssler Fiorenza's and Rosemary Ruether's insistence on seeing gender as socially constructed and men and women as the same, they nevertheless believe women's experience to be different than men's and assign an epistemological privilege to women church *(ekklesia gynaikon).*

29. Carter Heyward, *A Priest Forever: The Formation of a Woman and a Priest* (New York: Harper and Row, 1976), 32–33.

30. Leonora Tubbs Tisdale, "Women's Ways of Communicating: A New Blessing for Preaching," in Douglass and Kay, *Women, Gender and Christian Community,* 105.

31. Catherine A. Ziel, "Mother Tongue/Father Tongue: Gender-Linked Differences in Language Use and Their Influence on the Perceived Authority of the Preacher" (Ph.D. diss., Princeton Theological Seminary, 1991); Tisdale, "Women's Ways," 106–7.

32. Deborah Tannen, "The Power of Talk: Who Gets Heard and Why," *Harvard Business Review* (Sept./Oct. 1995): 137.

33. See Janet L. Weathers, "Gender and Small Group Communication in the Church," in *Women, Gender, and Christian Community,* and Tannen, *Gender and Discourse,* 9–10.

34. Madeleine L'Engle, "Bones," in *Rattling Those Dry Bones: Women Changing the Church,* ed. June Steffensen Hagen (San Diego: LuraMedia, 1995), 22.

35. Deborah Tannen, "Dangerous Women," review of *Woman's Inhumanity to Woman* by Phyllis Chesler, *The Washington Post* (March 10, 2002).

36. Phyllis Chesler, *Woman's Inhumanity to Woman* (New York: Thunder's Mouth Press, 2002).

37. Carpenter, *A Time For Honor,* 49.

38. Linda H. Hollies, *Bodacious Womanist Wisdom* (Cleveland: The Pilgrim Press, 2003), 23.

39. See Tanner, review of Chesler, *The Washington Post* (March 10, 2002).

40. L'Engle, "Bones," 21.

41. Rev. Rachel Lewis, interview, San Francisco, California, August 4, 2004.

42. Harrison Owen, *Open Space Technology: A User's Guide,* 2d ed. (San Francisco: Berrett-Koehler Publishers, 1997), 1, 15.

43. Gilbert R. Rendle, *Leading Change in the Congregation: Spiritual and Organizational Tools for Leaders*

(Washington, D.C.: The Alban Institute, 1998), 6.

44. Farris and Troxell, "One Eye on the Past," 44–45. www.womensordination.org.

45. Kenda Creasy Dean and Ron Foster, *The Godbearing Life: The Art of Soul Tending for Youth Ministry* (Nashville: Upper Room, 1998), 35.

46. Susan Willhauck, "Cultivating a Culture of the Call: A Model for Lay Theological Education," *Theological Education* 38, no. 2 (2002): 115.

47. Ibid., 115–16.

48. John Ackerman, *Listening to God: Spiritual Formation in Congregations* (The Alban Institute, 2001), 1, 4–5.

49. Nelson, "Prospecting," 32.

Chapter 3. Not Just Talking Heads: Biblical and Historical Perspectives on Back Talk!

1. For a helpful discussion of the dilemma, see Gérald Caron, "The Authority of the Bible Challenged by Feminist Hermeneutics," in *Women Also Journeyed With Him: Feminist Perspectives on the Bible,* eds. Gérald Caron et al. (Collegeville, Minn.: The Liturgical Press, 2000).

2. Ibid., 154, 156.

3. Ruether, *Sexism and God-Talk,* 23.

4. Caron, "Authority of the Bible," 154–56.

5. Loraine MacKenzie Shepherd, *Feminist Theologies for a Postmodern Church: Diversity, Community and Scripture* (New York: Peter Lang, 2002), 227–28.

6. Ibid.

7. Ibid., 98–99.

8. www.tifereth.org/ RABBI/ARCHIVE/5763/Pesach.htm.

9. Darrell J. Fasching, "Faith and Ethics after the Holocaust: What Christians Can Learn from the Jewish Narrative Tradition of Hutzpah," *Journal of Ecumenical Studies* 27, no. 3 (1990): 453, 455.

10. Ibid., 455, 461.

11. Belden C. Lane, "Hutzpa K'Lapei Shamaya: A Christian Response to the Jewish Tradition of Arguing with God," *Journal of Ecumenical Studies* 23, no. 4 (1986): 567.

12. Ibid., 569.

13. Ibid., 579, 580, 581.

14. Samuel E. Balentine, *Prayer in the Hebrew Bible: The Drama of Divine-Human Dialogue* (Minneapolis: Fortress Press, 1993), 4.

15. Ibid., 6, 261, 288.

16. Chopp, *Power to Speak,* 52.

17. Fasching, "Faith and Ethics," 455.

18. *New Interpreter's Bible,* vol. 1 (Nashville: Abingdon Press, 1994), 607.

19. http://www.firstpresnyc.org/sermons/2002/web/020707.html.

20. Joyce Hollyday, *Clothed with the Sun: Biblical Women Social Justice & Us* (Louisville: Westminster John Knox Press, 1994), 189, 141.

21. Katharine Doob Sakenfeld, "Numbers," in *The Women's Bible Commentary,* ed. Carol A. Newsom and Sharon H. Ringe (Louisville: Westminster/John Knox Press, 1992), 48.

22. Ibid.

23. Bruce C. Birch, Walter Brueggemann, et al., *A Theological Introduction to the Old Testament* (Nashville: Abingdon Press, 1999), 393.

24. Balentine, *Prayer in the Hebrew Bible,* 172.

25. Birch et al., *A Theological Introduction,* 402–3.

26. Denise Dombkowski Hopkins, *Journey Through the Psalms,* rev. ed. (St. Louis: Chalice Press, 2002), 77, 113.

27. Balentine, *Prayer in the Hebrew Bible,* 146.

28. Proctor-Smith, *Praying With Our Eyes Open,* 54.

29. Hopkins, *Journey Through the Psalms,* 113.

30. Tereza Cavalcanti, "The Prophetic Ministry of Women in the Hebrew Bible," in *Through Her Eyes: Women's Theology from Latin America,* ed. Elsa Tamez (New York: Orbis Books, 1989), 121–22.

31. Brueggerman quoted in Marcia Y. Riggs, ed., *Can I Get a Witness: Prophetic Religious Voices of African American Women An Anthology* (New York: Orbis Books, 1997), xii.

32. Hopkins, *Journey Through the Psalms,* 4.

33. According to the Catholic Encyclopedia Online edition, vol. VII, 2003, St. Thomas defined heresy as:

> *a species of infidelity in men who, having professed the faith of Christ, corrupt its dogmas. The right Christian faith consists in giving one's voluntary assent to Christ in all that truly belongs to His teaching. There are, therefore, two ways of deviating from Christianity: the one by refusing to believe in Christ Himself, which is the way of infidelity, common to Pagans and Jews; the other by restricting belief to certain points of Christ's doctrine selected and fashioned at pleasure, which is the way of heretics.*
> *(Summa Theologica II–II:11:1)*

Web site: http://www.newadvent.org.

34. Ruether and McLaughlin, *Women of Spirit,* 18.

35. Proctor-Smith, *Praying With Our Eyes Open,* 74.

36. Deborah F. Sawyer, *Women and Religion in the First Christian Centuries* (New York: Routledge, 1996), 2.

37. Ibid., 17.

38. Ibid., 36–37.

39. Ibid., 74, 77.

40. Karen Jo Torjesen, *When Women Were Priests: Women's Leadership in the Early Church and the Scandal of their Subordination in the Rise of Christianity* (San Francisco: Harper Collins, 1993), 11.

41. Sawyer, *Women and Religion,* 93, 96.

42. Barbara J. MacHaffie, *Her Story: Women in Christian Tradition* (Philadelphia: Fortress Press, 1986), 28.

43. Torjesen, *When Women Were Priests,* 8.

44. Joan Morris, *The Lady was a Bishop: The Hidden History of Women with Clerical Ordination and the Jurisdiction of Bishops* (New York: Macmillan Co., 1973).

45. Elisabeth Schüssler Fiorenza, *In Memory of Her: A Feminist Reconstruction of Christian Origins* (New York: Crossroad Publishing Co., 1983), 181.

46. Karen L. King, "Women in Ancient Christianity: The New Discoveries," in *From Jesus to Christ: The First Christians.* http://www.pbs.org/wgbh/pages/frontline/shows/religion/first/women.html.

47. Sawyer, *Women and Religion,* 99.

48. Ruether and McLaughlin, *Women of Spirit,* 20.

49. Karen L. King, see note 46 above.

50. Roger Gryson, *The Ministry of Women in the Early Church,* trans. Jean Laporte and Mary Louise Hall (Collegeville, Minn.: The Liturgical Press, 1976), 7.

51. MacHaffie, *Her Story,* 26.

52. Sawyer, *Women and Religion,* 42.

53. Ibid., 147.

54. Justo L. Gonzalez, *The Story of Christianity,* vol. 1, *The Early Church to the Dawn of the Reformation* (San Francisco: Harper and Row, 1984), 98.

55. MacHaffie, *Her Story,* 30.

56. Gryson, *Ministry,* 30, 32, 41–43. I am indebted to Debra Hanson for her summary in "Single Clergywomen Thriving in Ministry: Adapting the Model of the Quaker Clearness Committee For Discernment" (D. Min. project thesis, Wesley Theological Seminary, 2004).

57. Torjesen, *When Women Were Priests,* 93, 118.

58. Watson, *Feminist Theology,* 18–19.

59. MacHaffie, *Her Story,* 43–48.

60. For a discussion of these see ibid., 68–73.

61. Ruether and McLaughlin, *Women of Spirit,* 20.

62. MacHaffie, *Her Story,* 80–81, 84. Again, for an explanation of specific women leaders see MacHaffie, 84–91 and Delores C. Carpenter, *A Time For Honor: A Portrait of African American Clergywomen,* specifically note 23 to Chapter 1.

63. Nancy Hardesty, Lucille Sider Dayton, and Donald W. Dayton, "Women in the Holiness Movement: Feminism in the Evangelical Tradition," in Ruether and McLaughlin, *Women of Spirit,* 226, 254.

64. Barbara Brown Zikmund, "Women and Ordination," in *In Our Own Voices: Four Centuries of American Women's Religious Writing,* ed. Rosemary Skinner Keller and Rosemary Radford Ruether (Louisville: Westminster/John Knox Press, 1995), 295.

65. Ibid., 294. See also Anna Howard Shaw, *The Story of A Pioneer* (Cleveland: The Pilgrim Press, 1994).

66. Pamela W. Darling, *New Wine: The Story of Women Transforming Leadership and Power in the Episcopal Church* (Boston: Cowley Publications, 1994), 115.

67. See Darling for a fuller account, and see chapter five in this work for events leading up to the decision.

68. Told to me by Christina Rees, president of WATCH and member of the General Synod. Telephone interview, March 1, 2004.

69. Rosemary Radford Ruether, "Women and Roman Catholic Christianity," in *Women 2000: Gender, Equality, Development and Peace for the Twenty-First Century: The Holy See and the Fourth World Conference on Women Revisited* (Washington, D.C.: Catholics for a Free Choice, 2000), 9–10. Interestingly, during the Communist takeover of Czechoslovakia, a Catholic bishop ordained a woman (Ludmila Javorova) to serve as priest of an underground church. She may have been one of several women ordained for this purpose. http://www.womensordination.org.

70. Karl Rahner, *Concern for the Church,* vol. 20 of *Theological Investigations* (London: Darton, Longman and Todd, 1981), 40.

71. David Willis, "Women's Ordination: Can the Church Be Catholic Without it?" in Douglass and Kay, *Women, Gender, and Christian Community,* 88.

72. Chaves, *Ordaining Women,* 5.

73. Rosemary Ruether, "The Roman Catholic Story," in Ruether and

McLaughlin, *Women of Spirit,* 373–74.

74. Ruether, "Women and Roman Catholic Christianity," 10.

75. Ada María Isasi-Díaz, *Mujerista Theology* (New York: Orbis Books, 1996), 170–71.

76. Chopp, *Power to Speak,* 76.

77. Watson, *Feminist Theology*, 46. Teresa Berger provides a kaleidoscopic picture of women-identified liturgical communities all over the world in *Dissident Daughters: Feminist Liturgies in Global Context* (Louisville: Westminster John Knox Press, 2001).

78. Quoted in *Defecting in Place: Women Claiming Responsibility for Their Own Spiritual Lives* by Miriam Therese Winter, Adair Lummis, and Allison Stokes (New York: Crossroad Press, 1995), 114.

79. Ruether, "Women and Roman Catholic Christianity," 11.

Chapter 4. Talking Us Through It: Stories and Strategies for Change

1. Chopp, *Power to Speak,* 2.

2. Procter-Smith, *Praying With Our Eyes Open,* 13–14.

3. Rev. Dr. Janice Jenkins points out that Baptists are a collection of autonomous churches, and while she makes some generalizations about the denomination of which she is a lifelong member, she does not intend to speak for all Baptists.

4. Janice Stancil Jenkins, "Ordination of Women in the Northern Virginia Baptist Association: The Difference Four Years Makes" (D.Min thesis, Wesley Theological Seminary, April 2002).

5. Rev. Dr. Janice Jenkins was licensed to preach and ordained in her denomination.

6. Carpenter, *A Time For Honor,* 15.

7. Maria Harris, *Fashion Me a People: Curriculum in the Church* (Louisville: Westminster John Knox Press, 1989), 27.

8. John P. Kotter, *Leading Change: The Eight Steps to Transformation* (Boston: Harvard Business School Press, 1996), 35–49.

9. Patricia Farris, "Creating a Collaborative Culture" in *Best Practices from America's Best Churches,* ed. Paul Wilkes and Marty Minchin (New York: Paulist Press, 2003), 123–25.

10. hooks, *Talking Back,* 9, 28.

11. Stephen Carter, *The Culture of Disbelief: How American Law and Politics Trivialize Religious Devotion* (New York: Anchor Books, 1994).

12. Kelly Brown Douglas, *Sexuality and the Black Church* (New York: Orbis Books, 1999), 19–21.

13. Kellerman, "You've Come a Long Way Baby," 58.

14. Donald Barnes, "Still Far to Go," in *Voices of this Calling: Experiences of the First Generation of Women Priests,* ed. Christina Rees (Norwich: Canterbury Press, 2002), 48.

15. Rev. Bernice Broggio quoted in *Jobs for the Boys: Women Who Became Priests,* eds. Liz and Andrew Barr (London: Hodder and Stoughton, 2001), 75.

16. Chaves, *Ordaining Women,* 173–74.

17. Kotter, *Leading Change,* 51–66.

18. Ibid., 102–6.

19. Christina Rees, telephone interview, March 1, 2004.

20. Jean Miller Schmidt, "Reexamining the Public/Private Split: Reforming the Continent and Spreading Scriptural Holiness," in Russell Richey, Kenneth Rowe, Jean

Miller Schmidt, eds., *Perspectives on American Methodism* (Nashville: Abingdon Press, 1993), 244.

21. Shepherd, *Feminist Theologies,* 94.

22. Kwok Pui-lan, "God Weeps with Our Pain," in *New Eyes for Reading Biblical and Theological Reflections by Women from the Third World,* ed. John S. Pobee and Bärbel Von Wartenberg-Potter (Geneva: World Council of Churches, 1986).

23. Procter-Smith, *Praying With Our Eyes Open,* 38.

24. Kotter, *Leading Change,* 104–6.

25. Quoted in Becker, *Leading Women,* 68.

26. Procter-Smith, *Praying With Our Eyes Open,* 38.

27. Ruether, *Sexism and God-Talk,* 265.

28. hooks, *Talking Back,* 20.

29. Joan Chittister, *The Friendship of Women: A Spiritual Tradition* (Erie, Pa.: Sheed and Ward, 2000), 11–12.

30. Max DePree, *Leadership is an Art* (New York: Dell Publishing, 1989), 81–82.

31. Chittister, *Friendship of Women,* 15, 30.

32. Pui-lan, *Introducing Asian Feminist Theology,* 107.

33. United Methodist News Service, March 31, 2004. http://www.umc.org.

34. Jeanne Porter, *Leading Ladies: Transformative Biblical Images for Women's Leadership* (Philadelphia, Pa.: Innisfree Press, 2000), 20.

35. Lucy Winkett, "Facing the Light," in Rees, *Voices of this Calling,* 196.

36. Darling, *New Wine,* 115.

37. Sue Hiatt died May 30, 2002. She was the John Seely Stone Professor of Pastoral Theology at Episcopal Divinity School.

38. Darling, *New Wine,* 119–20.

39. Ibid., 124.

40. Ibid., 123.

41. Ibid., 131.

42. The eleven were: Merrill Bittner, Alla Bozarth-Campbell, Allison Cheek, Emily Hewitt, Carter Heyward, Suzanne Hiatt, Marie Moorefield, Jeannette Piccard, Beth Bone Schiess, Katrina Welles Swanson, and Nancy Hatch Wittig. For data and analysis on female Episcopal priests see http://andromeda.rutgers.edu/~lcrew/womenpr.html (Web site by Dr. Louie Crews, Rutgers University).

43. Procter-Smith, *Praying With Our Eyes Open,* 41.

44. http://www.womensordination.org.

45. Chaves, *Ordaining Women,* 171.

46. Miriam Therese Winter, "Feminist Women's Spirituality: Breaking New Ground in the Church" in Johnson, *The Church Women Want,* 25.

Chapter 5. Too Much Talk: The Limits of Talk in Creating Change

1. Chopp, *Power to Speak,* 25.

2. Alvin John Schmidt, *Veiled and Silenced: How Culture Shaped Sexist Theology* (Macon, Ga.: Mercer University Press, 1989), 132.

3. Deborah Cameron, *Feminism and Linguistic Theory* (London: Macmillan Press, 1985), 171–73.

4. Katie Geneva Cannon, *Black Womanist Ethics* (Atlanta: Scholars Press, 1988), 42.

5. Douglas, *Sexuality and the Black Church,* 68.

6. Cameron, *Feminism and Linguistic Theory,* 105.

7. Elke Betz-Schmidt, interview, Baltimore, Maryland, April 17, 2004.

8. Department of Justice Office on Violence Against Women http://www.ojp.usdoj.gov/vawo. See also the National Organization for Women http://www.now.org.

9. Ellen Goodman, "Unfriendly Fires in the Gender Wars," *The Washington Post,* April 10, 2004.

10. Department of Justice Office on Violence Against Women http://www.ojp.usdoj.gov/vawo. Many young boys and men are also victims in the international sex-trafficking industry.

11. http://www.asiafoundation.org/ Women/violence.html.

12. Bernadette Mbuy Beya, "Women in the Church in Africa: Possibilities for Presence and Promises," in *Talitha cum! Theologies of African Women,* ed. Myambura J. Njoroge and Musa W. Dube (South Africa: Cluster Publications, 2001), 185.

13. United Methodist News Service, March 31, 2004. http://www.umc.org

14. Michelle A. Gonzalez, *Sor Juana: Beauty and Justice in the Americas* (New York: Maryknoll Press, 2003), 1, 3, 5, 33.

15. Cameron, *Feminism and Linguistic Theory,* 158, 160.

16. Sharon H. Ringe, "Reading from Context to Context: Contributions of a Feminist Hermeneutic to Theologies of Liberation," in *Lift Every Voice: Constructing Christian Theologies from the Underside,* ed. Susan Brooks Thistlethwaite and Mary Potter Engel (New York: Orbis Books, 1998), 290.

17. Roger J. Vanden Busch, "The Value of Silence in Quaker Spirituality," *Spirituality Today* (Winter 1985): 326–35.

18. United Methodist News service, March 31, 2004. http://www.umc.

Chapter 6. Back Talk on the Frontline

1. Joan D. Chittister, *Scarred by Struggle, Transformed by Hope* (Grand Rapids, Mich.: Eerdmans Publishing Co., 2003), 24.

2. Diana Hayes, "Speaking the Future into Life: The Challenge of Black Women in the Church," in Johnson, *The Church Women Want,* 90.

3. Miriam Therese Winter, "Feminist Women's Spirituality: Breaking New Ground in the Church," in Johnson, *The Church Women Want,* 31.

4. Caroline Dick, "Ongoing Transformation," in Rees, *Voices of this Calling,* 168.

BIBLIOGRAPHY

Ackerman, John. *Listening to God: Spiritual Formation in Congregations.* The Alban Institute, 2001.

Ashe, Kaye. *The Feminization of the Church?* Kansas City, Mo.: Sheed and Ward, 1997.

Balentine, Samuel E. *Prayer in the Hebrew Bible: The Drama of Divine-Human Dialogue.* Minneapolis: Fortress Press, 1993.

Barr, Liz, and Andrew Barr, eds. *Jobs for the Boys: Women Who Became Priests.* London: Hodder and Stoughton, 2001.

Becker, Carol E. *Leading Women: How Church Women Can Avoid Leadership Traps and Negotiate the Gender Maze.* Nashville: Abingdon Press, 1996.

Berger, Teresa, ed. *Dissident Daughters: Feminist Liturgies in Global Context.* Louisville: Westminster John Knox Press, 2001.

Birch, Bruce, Walter Brueggemann, et al., eds. *A Theological Introduction to the Old Testament.* Nashville: Abingdon Press, 1999.

Cameron, Deborah. *Feminism and Linguistic Theory.* London: Macmillan Press, 1985.

Cannon, Katie Geneva. *Black Womanist Ethics.* Atlanta: Scholars Press, 1988.

Caron, Gérald et al., eds. *Women Also Journeyed with Him: Feminist Perspectives on the Bible.* Collegeville, Minn.: The Liturgical Press, 2000.

Carpenter, Delores C. *A Time For Honor: A Portrait of African American Clergywomen.* St. Louis: Chalice Press, 2001.

Carter, Stephen. *The Culture of Disbelief: How American Law and Politics Trivialize Religious Devotion.* New York: Anchor Books, 1994.

Chaves, Mark. *Ordaining Women: Culture and Conflict in Religious Organizations.* Cambridge: Harvard University Press, 1997.

Chesler, Phyllis. *Woman's Inhumanity to Woman.* New York: Thunder's Mouth Press, 2002.

Chittister, Joan. *The Friendship of Women: A Spiritual Tradition.* Erie, Pa.: Sheed and Ward, 2000.

————. *Scarred by Struggle, Transformed by Hope.* Grand Rapids, Mich.: Eerdmans Publishing Co., 2003.

————. *Winds of Change: Women Challenge the Church.* Kansas City, Mo.: Sheed and Ward, 1986.

Chopp, Rebecca S. *The Power to Speak: Feminism, Language, God.* New York: Crossroad Publishing Co., 1989.

Congar, Jay, et al. *The Leadership Change Handbook: An Essential Guide to Setting Direction and Taking Action.* San Francisco: Harper and Row, 1999.

Crittenden, Danielle. "Let's Junk the Feminist Slogans: The War's Over." *Chatelaine* (August 1989): 38.

Cueni, R. Robert. *Dinosaur Heart Transplants: Renewing Mainline Congregations.* Nashville: Abingdon Press, 2000.

Darling, Pamela W. *New Wine: The Story of Women Transforming Leadership and Power in the Episcopal Church.* Boston: Cowley Publications, 1994.

Dean, Kenda, and Ron Foster. *The Godbearing Life: The Art of Soul Tending for Youth Ministry.* Nashville: Upper Room, 1998.

Delorey, Ann. "Conservative Renewal Movements and the Threat to the Liberative Power of the Christian Tradition for Women in the Presbyterian Church USA." M.T.S. Thesis, Wesley Theological Seminary, 2001.

Dempsey Douglass, Jane and James F. Kay, eds. *Women, Gender, and Christian Community.* Louisville: Westminster John Knox Press, 1997.

DePree, Max. *Leadership is an Art.* New York: Dell Publishing, 1989.

Donovan, Mary S. *A Different Call: Women's Ministries in the Episcopal Church, 1850–1920.* Harrisburg, Pa. Morehouse Publishing, 1986.

Douglas, Kelly Brown. *Sexuality and the Black Church.* New York: Orbis Books, 1999.

Everist, Norma Cook. *Ordinary Ministry, Extraordinary Challenge: Women and the Roles of Ministry.* Nashville: Abingdon Press, 2000.

Faludi, Susan. *Backlash: The Undeclared War Against American Women.* New York: Anchor Books, 1991.

Farris, Patricia, and Barbara Troxell. "Women's Contribution to Church Renewal." *Quarterly Review* 18 (Spring 1998): 37–53.

Fasching, Darrell J. "Faith and Ethics after the Holocaust: What Christians Can Learn from the Jewish Narrative Tradition of Hutzpah." *Journal of Ecumenical Studies* 27, no. 3 (1990): 453–79.

Finger, Reta Halteman, and Kari Sandhaas, eds. *The Wisdom of Daughters: Two Decades of the Voice of Christian Feminism.* Philadelphia: Innisfree Press, 2001.

Gonzalez, Justo L. *The Story of Christianity.* Vol. 1, *The Early Church to the Dawn of the Reformation.* San Francisco: Harper and Row, 1984.

Gonzalez, Michelle A. *Sor Juana: Beauty and Justice in the Americas.* New York: Maryknoll Press, 2003.

Goodman, Ellen. "Unfriendly Fires in the Gender Wars." *The Washington Post,* April 10, 2004.

Grey, Mary C. *Beyond the Dark Night: A Way Forward for the Church?* London: Cassell, 1997.

Groome, Thomas. *Educating for Life: A Spiritual Vision for Every Teacher and Parent.* Allen, Tex.: Thomas More, 1998.

Gryson, Roger. *The Ministry of Women in the Early Church.* Translated by Jean Laporte and Mary Louise Hall. Collegeville, Minn.: The Liturgical Press, 1976.

Guder, Darrell L. *The Continuing Conversion of the Church.* Grand Rapids, Mich.: William B. Eerdmans Press, 2000.

Hagan, June Steffensen, ed. *Rattling Those Dry Bones: Women Changing the Church.* San Diego: LuraMedia, 1995.

Hanson, Debra. "Single Clergywomen Thriving in Ministry: Adapting the Model of the Quaker Clearness Committee For Discernment." D.Min. Project Thesis. Wesley Theological Seminary, 2004.

Harris, Maria. *Fashion Me a People: Curriculum in the Church.* Louisville: Westminster John Knox Press, 1989.

Hayes, Diana L. *Hagar's Daughters: Womanist Ways of Being in the World.* New York: Paulist Press, 1995.

Heilbrun, Carolyn. *Writing a Woman's Life.* New York: Ballantine Books, 1988.

Helgesen, Sally. *The Web of Inclusion: A New Architecture for Building Great Organizations.* New York: Doubleday, 1995.

Herrington, Jim, et al., eds. *Leading Congregational Change: A Practical Guide for the Transformational Journey.* San Francisco: Jossey-Bass, 2000.

Heyward, Carter. *Staying Power: Reflections on Gender, Justice and Compassion.* Cleveland, Ohio: The Pilgrim Press, 1995.

———. *A Priest Forever: The Formation of a Woman and a Priest.* San Francisco: Harper and Row, 1976.

Hollies, Linda H. *Bodacious Womanist Wisdom.* Cleveland: The Pilgrim Press, 2003.

Hollyday, Joyce. *Clothed with the Sun: Biblical Women Social Justice & Us.* Louisville: Westminster John Knox Press, 1994.

hooks, bell. *Feminist Theory: From Margin to Center.* Boston: South End Press, 1984.

———. *Talking Back: Thinking Feminist, Thinking Black.* Boston: South End Press, 1989.

Hopkins, Denise Dombkowski. *Journey Through the Psalms.* Rev. ed. St. Louis: Chalice Press, 2002.

Isasi-Diaz, Ada-Maria. *Mujerista Theology.* New York: Orbis Books, 1996.

———. *Mujerista Theology: A Theology for the Twenty-first Century.* Louisville: Westminster John Knox Press, 1996.

Isasi-Diaz, Ada-Maria, and Fernando Segovia. *Hispanic/Latino Theology: Challenge and Promise.* Philadelphia: Fortress Press, 1996.

Jacobsen, Dennis. *Doing Justice: Congregations and Community Organizing.* Minneapolis: Fortress Press, 2001.

Jenkins, Janice Stancil. "Ordination of Women in the Northern Virginia Baptist Association: The Difference Four Years Makes." D.Min. Thesis. Wesley Theological Seminary, 2002.

Johnson, Elizabeth A., ed. *The Church Women Want: Catholic Women in Dialogue.* New York: Crossroad Publishing Co., 2002.

Jordon, Judith V., ed. *Women's Growth in Diversity.* New York: The Guilford Press, 1971.

Kallestad, Walt. *Turn Your Church Inside Out: Building a Community for Others.* Minneapolis: Augsburg/Fortress Press, 2001.

Keller, Rosemary Skinner and Rosemary Radford Ruether, eds. *In Our Own Voices: Four Centuries of American Women's Religious Writing.* Louisville: Westminster John Knox Press, 1995.

Kim, Grace Ji-Sun. *A Korean North American Women's Christology.* Cleveland: The Pilgrim Press, 2002.

Kotter, John P. *Leading Change: The Eight Steps to Transformation.* Boston: Harvard Business School Press, 1996.

Kwok Pui-lan. "God Weeps with Our Pain." *New Eyes for Reading Biblical and Theological Reflections by Women from the Third World,* eds. John S. Pobee and Bärbel Von Wartenberg-Potter. Geneva: World Council of Churches, 1986.

———. *Introducing Asian Feminist Theology.* Cleveland: The Pilgrim Press, 2000.

Lane, Belden C. "Hutzpa K'Lapei Shamaya: A Christian Response to the Jewish Tradition of Arguing with God," *Journal of Ecumenical Studies* 23, no. 4 (1986): 567–86.

MacHaffie, Barbara J. *Her Story: Women in Christian Tradition.* Philadelphia: Fortress Press, 1986.

Mascia-Lees, Frances and Sharpe, Patricia. *Taking a Stand in a Postfeminist World: Toward an Engaged Cultural Criticism.* New York: State University of New York Press, 2000.

Matthews, John R. *Are Women Clergy Changing the Nature and Practice of Ministry?* Columbus: The Midwest Ministry Development Service, 1996.

McKenzie, Vashtie. *Not Without a Struggle: Leadership Development for African American Women in Ministry.* Cleveland: United Church Press, 1996.

———. *Strength in the Struggle: Leadership Development for Women.* Cleveland: The Pilgrim Press, 2001.

Milk, Leslie. "Girls Rule." *The Washingtonian Magazine,* September 2001.

Mitchem, Stephanie. *Introducing Womanist Theology.* New York: Orbis Books, 2002.

Morris, Joan. *The Lady was a Bishop: The Hidden History of Women with Clerical Ordination and the Jurisdiction of Bishops.* New York: Macmillan Co., 1973.

Newsom, Carol A., and Sharon H. Ringe, eds. *The Women's Bible Commentary.* Louisville: Westminster John Knox Press, 1992.

Owen, Harrison. *Open Space Technology: A User's Guide.* San Francisco: Berrett-Koehler Publishers, Inc., 1997.

Patterson, Sheron C. *New Faith: A Black Christian Woman's Guide to Reformation, Re-creation, Rediscovery, Renaissance, Resurrection, and Revival.* Minneapolis: Fortress Press, 2000.

Porter, Jeanne. *Leading Ladies: Transformative Biblical Images for Women's Leadership.* Philadelphia: Innisfree Press, 2000.

Procter-Smith, Marjorie. *Praying With Our Eyes Open: Engendering Feminist Liturgical Prayer.* Nashville: Abingdon Press. 1995.

Rahner, Karl. *Theological Investigations.* Vol. 20. London: Darton, Longman and Todd, 1981.

Rees, Christina, ed. *Voices of this Calling: Experiences of the First Generation of Women Priests.* Norwich: Canterbury Press, 2002.

Rendle, Gilbert R. *Leading Change in the Congregation: Spiritual and Organizational Tools for Leaders.* Washington, D.C.: The Alban Institute, 1998.

Riggs, Marcia Y., ed. *Can I Get a Witness? Prophetic Religious Voices of African American Women: An Anthology.* New York: Orbis Books, 1997.

Rhode, Deborah L., ed. *The Difference Difference Makes: Women and Leadership.* Stanford: Calif.: Stanford University Press, 2003.

Ruether, Rosemary. *Sexism and God-Talk: Toward a Feminist Theology.* Boston: Beacon Press, 1993.

————. "Women and Roman Catholic Christianity." *Women 2000: Gender, Equality, Development and Peace for the Twenty-First Century: The Holy See and the Fourth World Conference on Women Revisited.* Washington, D.C.: Catholics for a Free Choice, 2000.

Ruether, Rosemary, and Eleanor McLaughlin, eds. *Women of Spirit: Female Leadership in the Jewish and Christian Traditions.* Eugene, Ore.: Wipf and Stock Publishers, 1998.

Russell, Letty, M. *Church in the Round: Feminist Interpretation of the Church.* Louisville: Westminster/John Knox Press, 1993.

Sawyer, Deborah F. *Women and Religion in the First Christian Centuries.* New York: Routledge, 1996.

Schmidt, Alvin John. *Veiled and Silenced: How Culture Shaped Sexist Theology.* Macon, Ga.: Mercer University Press., 1989.

Schüssler Fiorenza, Elisabeth. *In Memory of Her: A Feminist Reconstruction of Christian Origins.* New York: Crossroad Publishing Co., 1983.

Shepherd, Loraine MacKenzie. *Feminist Theologies for a Postmodern Church: Diversity, Community and Scripture.* New York: Peter Lang, 2002.

Spencer, Liz. "Precious Daughters: Faith Stories of Clergywomen of the Virginia Annual Conference." Unpublished document. 2001.

Tamez, Elsa, ed. *Through Her Eyes: Women's Theology from Latin America.* New York: Orbis Books, 1989.

Tannen, Deborah. "Dangerous Women." Review of *Woman's Inhumanity to Woman. The Washington Post,* March 10, 2002.

————. *Gender and Discourse.* New York: Oxford University Press, 1994.

————. "The Power of Talk: Who Gets Heard and Why." *Harvard Business Review* (Sept./Oct. 1995): 139–48.

Thistletwaite, Susan Brooks, and Mary Potter Engel, eds. *Lift Every Voice: Constructing Christian Theologies from the Underside.* New York: Orbis Books. 1998.

Torjesen, Karen Jo. *When Women Were Priests: Women's Leadership in the Early Church and the Scandal of their Subordination in the Rise of Christianity.* San Francisco: Harper Collins, 1993.

Vanden Busch, Roger J. "The Value of Silence in Quaker Spirituality." *Spirituality Today* (Winter 1985): 326–35.

Van Scoyoc, Nancy J. *Women, Change, and the Church.* Nashville: Abingdon Press, 1980.

Warren, Michael, ed. *Changing Churches: The Local Church and the Structures of Change.* Portland, Ore.: Pastoral Press, 2000.

Watson, Natalie K. *Feminist Theology.* Grand Rapids: Eerdmans Publishing Co., 2003.

Wijngaards, John. *The Ordination of Women in the Catholic Tradition: Unmasking a Cuckoo's Egg Tradition.* New York: Continuum, 2001.

Wilkes, Paul, and Marty Minchin, eds. *Best Practices from America's Best Churches.* New York: Paulist Press, 2003.

Willhauck, Susan. "Cultivating a Culture of the Call: A Model for Lay Theological Education." *Theological Education* (2002): 111–25.

Willhauck, Susan, and Jacqulyn Thorpe. *The Web of Women's Leadership: Recasting Congregational Ministry.* Nashville: Abingdon Press, 2001.

Williams, Delores S. *Sisters in the Wilderness: The Challenge of Womanist God-Talk.* New York: Orbis Books, 1995.

Winter, Miriam Therese, et al. *Defecting in Place: Women Claiming Responsibility for Their Own Spiritual Lives.* New York: Crossroad Press, 1995.

INDEX